MW00323715

BEFORE WE SAY GOODBYE

PRACTICAL GUIDANCE, INSPIRING STORIES AND PRAYERS TO HELP US PREPARE A GOOD DEATH

Ray Simpson

HarperCollins*Publishers*

Permission has been sought for all quoted material
in this book. The publishers will gladly insert
further acknowledgements in any future edition.

HarperCollins *Religious*
Part of HarperCollinsPublishers
77–85 Fulham Palace Road, London w6 8jb
www.christian-publishing.com

First published in Great Britain in 2001
by HarperCollinsReligious

1 3 5 7 9 10 8 6 4 2

Copyright © 2001 Ray Simpson

Ray Simpson asserts the moral right to
be identified as the author of this work

A catalogue record for this book
is available from the British Library

ISBN 0 00 711939 9

Printed and bound in Great Britain by
Creative Print and Design (Wales), Ebbw Vale

CONDITIONS OF SALE
This book is sold subject to the condition that it shall not,
by way of trade or otherwise, be lent, re-sold, hired out or
otherwise circulated without the publisher's prior consent
in any form of binding or cover other than that in which it
is published and without a similar condition including this
condition being imposed on the subsequent purchaser.

All rights reserved. No part of this publication may be
reproduced, stored in a retrieval system, or transmitted,
in any form or by any means, electronic, mechanical,
photocopying, recording or otherwise, without the prior
permission of the publishers.

A well rounded life should have a beginning, a middle and an end.
MURRAY PARKES

Spirit of the Holy Flame
The blowing wind
The burning cloud

Guard us on each lonely path
Between our birth and death
Our sparrow flight
And light us home
FROM ST AIDAN'S CHAPEL, BRADFORD CATHEDRAL

CONTENTS

* * *

ACKNOWLEDGEMENTS

Canterbury Press, Norwich for permission to use J. Philip Newell's prayer *As it was in the stillness of the morning* ... taken from *Celtic Benediction*; Marilyn MacCallum for permission to tell the story of her late husband Colin, based on her notes; Brian Frost for permission to use his poem *Farewell my lovely friends*; Michael Halliwell for permission to use his poem *Lord of the sunrise*; Bishop Mael of the Celtic Orthodox Church, Saint Dol for permission to use his prayer *My good angel, messenger of God*; Kevin Mayhew Ltd for G. Markland's hymn *Do not be afraid*, used by permission from *Hymns Old and New*, Licence No. 106031; Stephen J. Palmer for permission to use the poem *Let go of summer* from his book *The Words My Hands Could Not Write* ISBN 0-9512344-7-1; Noel Proctor for permission to use extracts from the diary of his late wife, Norma; SPCK for permission to use *Ebb tide, full tide* from David Adam's *The Edge of Glory*; Stainer & Bell Ltd, London, England for permission to use an extract from *Lord of the Dance* by Sydney Carter; Transworld Publishers for extracts from *Anam Cara* by John O'Donohue; Glynn and Mandy Walker for permission to use their material on the death of their baby Eleanor, the 'Sweet Pea'; The Wild Goose Resource Group for permission to quote from the two songs All the fears I need to name by John Bell, copyright © 1997 WGRG, Iona Community, 840 Govan Road, Glasgow G51 3UU, from 'The Last Journey: songs for the time of grieving' (Wild Goose Publications, Glasgow, 1997), and The last journey, by John L. Bell & Graham Maule, copyright © 1988 WGRG Iona Community, 840 Govan Road, Glasgow G51 3UU, from 'The Last Journey: songs for the time of grieving' (Wild Goose Publications, Glasgow, 1997). Also for permission to quote from George McLeod's *A veil thin as gossamer* in his *The Whole Earth Shall Cry Glory*; Extracts from the *Carmina Gadelica* are taken from the edition published by Floris Books; Quotations from *Hebridean Altars* by Alistair Maclean are taken from the book of that title published by The Moray Press, Edinburgh and London in 1937; Quotations from the Bible are from The New Revised Standard Version (Anglicised Edition) copyright 1989, 1995 by the Division of Christian Education of the National Council of the Churches of Christ in the United States of America or are the author's own translation.

IMPORTANT NOTE

Throughout this book spaces are provided in which readers can write their wishes for themselves and their affairs before and after death. These should be treasured and made available to those who will need to see them. Readers may therefore wish to present a second copy of this book, also containing their written notes, to their executor or confidante. Alternatively, they may give photocopies of the appropriate pages to those concerned.

FOREWORD

by Jean Peart

I am so grateful to God for leading me to this book, and so grateful to Ray for writing it. It was such a help and comfort to me when my dear mother was dying. The prayers in this book gave reassurance, comfort and confidence as I stayed with my mother during her last weeks to continually pray over her and, I believe, to ease her passage to heaven.

My mother's passing was so peaceful and gentle (just like a candle going out). She indeed had death without pain, death without fear, death without death. A quote that has spoken to me over the last year is this: 'One should spend one's life contemplating one's deathbed.' Even the staff at the nursing home were amazed at the wonderful passing my mother had. The peace at the time of her passing and afterwards in the nursing home was like a blanket of peace that descended over the whole place for several hours.

This book is both deeply spiritual and very practical – a wonderful aid for those who care. I kept it in my handbag for a month, and sat with it in my hand through the last days with my mother.

May God bless and keep all who use this book.

Jean Peart
The Open Gate
The Holy Island of Lindisfarne

INTRODUCTION

Life is a journey from the womb to the tomb.
There are things to learn that make the journey, even at its end,
   worthwhile.
To live well requires us to die well.
If we are to die well, we need to prepare for it.
We are all dying. Some of us die sooner than others.
·The best time to start to prepare for death is when we are young.
Please don't die without having lived.
Please don't depart without having said truly satisfying goodbyes.

The airliner went into a nose dive. A maniac had attacked the pilot and broken the autopilot. Every passenger was convinced they were plunging to certain death. Lady Anabel Goldsmith was on that plane. In seats behind her were her son Zak, her daughter Jemima Khan, and her grandchildren. A myriad things she would have liked to have said and done before they parted this life flashed through her mind, but it seemed too late now. She had time to utter only one word to them: 'Goodbye.' By some miracle the plane, only seconds from disaster, was saved. Lady Anabel was given a second chance to get things right before she said goodbye.

This book offers us a chance to get things right before we say goodbye. It may be our only chance. Although we can run away from almost anything in life, we cannot run away from death. So much has been written about how to cope with other people's deaths. So little has been written about preparing for our own death. Those books that have been written are not the sort you would hold in your hand, or keep in your heart, when you are too weak to take in new information. This simple, practical guide comes from one heart to another. It calls us to live and to die well, to be good stewards of our short time on earth.

There are as many ways of dying as there are people. This little book will help you to plan your final journey, your farewells, your funeral and your will in a way that will uniquely bless you and those around you. Some are too fearful or thoughtless to do this. This book will help you to do it gently, in small doses.

Dying itself is a journey. We cannot halt it, but we may influence the spirit in which we make it. We can learn from enlightened people who have made glorious exits. We can learn from practitioners who have studied the cycles of dying. We can learn from the caring insights of the hospice movement. And now that hospital and funeral services are business oriented, we can be part of a citizens' movement to take back responsibility for our own and our loved ones' departures.

THE THINGS THEY SAY ABOUT DYING

To die well is the chief part of virtue.

GREEK PROVERB

A good death does honour to a whole life.

ITALIAN PROVERB

It is a great *art* to die well, and to be learned by those in health.

JEREMY TAYLOR, *The Rule and Exercises of Holy Dying*, 1651

Death can cause a human being to become what he or she was called to become; it can be, in the fullest sense of the word, an accomplishment.

FRANCOIS MITTERAND

Death, so far from being cruel, is an act of love rounding off our brief testing here.

ELIZABETH MYERS

It is impossible that anything so natural, so necessary, and so universal as death should ever have been designed by Providence as an evil.

JONATHAN SWIFT

Lord, grant that my last hour may be my best hour.

OLD ENGLISH PRAYER

If you would endure life, be prepared for death.

SIGMUND FREUD

Prepare for your death.

ST COLUMBA

When we are dead, and people weep for us and grieve, let it be because we touched their lives with beauty and simplicity.
JACOB P. RUDIN

Is there not a certain satisfaction in the fact that natural limits are set to the life of the individual, so that at the conclusion it may appear as a work of art?
ALBERT EINSTEIN

In this world nothing can be said to be certain, except death and taxes.
BENJAMIN FRANKLIN

Dying is like being stuck in a traffic jam.
There is a crown for those who endure.
ANON

Blessed be God for our sister, the death of the body.
ST FRANCIS OF ASSISI

Death is the great adventure beside which moon landings and space trips pale into insignificance.
JOSEPH BAYLY

*

Mortal loss is an Immortal gain.
The ruins of time builds Mansions in Eternity.
WILLIAM BLAKE

PART ONE

* * *

BEFRIEND DEATH
WHEN YOU ARE YOUNG

What's brave, what's noble,
Let's do it after the high Roman fashion,
And make death proud to take us.

WILLIAM SHAKESPEARE,
Antony and Cleopatra, ACT IV, SCENE 16

THERE'S A TIME TO
GIVE AND A TIME TO GO

For everything there is a season,
and a time for every matter under heaven:
a time to be born, and a time to die;
a time to plant, and a time to pluck up...
a time to seek, and a time to lose.

ECCLESIASTES 3:1,2,6 NRSV

The advice that most shaped me as a young man was this: Do not waste your life on empty pleasures or burn out prematurely for some great idea; let your life be like a candle, which gives of itself consistently until, when it has given all it has, it flickers out.

I want to give the best that I have at every stage of life. In order to give my best, I must also learn to receive from others at every level of my being. When I have given all that I have to give, and received all that I have to receive, I will flicker out in a glow of fulfilment.

Of course, none of us will achieve this 100 per cent, but it is good to aim for it. We will learn through trial and error. Life affords us opportunities to learn from our mistakes and, whatever our failings, to increase our levels of giving and receiving.

If we live like this, dying can feel like fulfilment rather than theft.

THE SECRET OF LIFE IS
THE SECRET OF DEATH

To live and die well – this is surely the supreme aim. I used to think that I might do one, or neither, but certainly not both. Now I know that the secret of one is also the secret of the other.

A professional rugby player told me that the secret of being a successful player is to go all out, to keep your eye on the ball, and not to hold back through fear of injury or failure.

Some people go all out in life, but they mess it up because they do not keep their eye on the ball – they lose sight of the end of life. Others hold back because they fear they will get hurt or fail.

I used to hold back because I feared I might lose my security or status. A counsellor advised me to visualize the worst scenario that could happen to me. I did so. Then he challenged me to face that worst scenario. I did so. Having faced it, I became willing to go through with it. Even though the worst scenario did not occur, facing it set me free to live fully in any scenario.

It is like that with life. Death stalks us as an unconscious paralyser, even when we are young. If we face this worst scenario of death now, it frees us to live at our maximum throughout our lives.

If we live fully, we shall die fulfilled.

If we are champions in life, we shall be champions in death.

DEATH PUTS LIFE
IN PERSPECTIVE

You may think you can get away with anything, that nothing can touch you, not even death. This ability to get away with things may seem to be your pride and glory.

The truth is, you will have to submit to death as surely as seed, once it is fully grown as wheat, is cut down and ground into flour. ECHOING ISAIAH 28

The prophet Isaiah believed God was speaking along these lines to 'successful' people who never gave a thought to anything or anyone else.

It is better to sow seeds of wheat rather than wild oats now, so that these will bring a good harvest in the future. Only so will the harvest of our lives be a good experience.

What you sow, you reap. What you give out, you receive back.

Living our life in the light of eternity gives us perspective. It sorts out our priorities.

WHEN FACED,
DEATH BUILDS VALOUR

A parent whose baby died said this: 'Our baby's death made me realize how thin and fragile are the surface things of life which we rely upon. Our baby's death made me less tolerant of arrogance. It made me value respect.'

A daring hit-and-run robber named Moses, who had killed people in pursuit of his crimes, reformed his life and lived as a hermit in the desert. He became a soul friend to young people, who joined him in the desert.

One day his desert brothers learned that an armed band was on its way to loot their dwellings and leave them for dead. They urged that everyone should make a quick escape.

'I'll stay here,' Moses said. 'I have waited so long for this day. My death will be a fitting reminder of Jesus' saying, "Those who use the sword shall die by the sword."'

In fact, the murderers arrived before any of them could escape. Seven brothers were killed.

There was one brother, however, who was not in the hut with them. He hid under some palm fronds and observed how they died. He saw seven crowns, each one coming to rest on the head of a brother.

Olympic athletes who know that a medal awaits the winner go all out. To know that there is a crown stirs us to valour – to good deeds, heroic acts, unstinting service, and to the noble bearing of suffering.

THE ACHE INSIDE US

Deep inside every human being there is an ache. We can try to drown it in restless activity, drug it with addictive substances, or isolate it by putting up defences. If we do this, our life becomes sound and fury, signifying nothing.

One philosopher describes this ache as 'the existential loneliness'. This ache may become acute when someone close to us dies, or in the season of falling leaves and encroaching dark, or when we leave behind some familiar part of our lives, or when we find ourselves alone.

It may even throb when something triggers a sense of mystery – we fall in love, we give birth to a child, we observe a glory of creation, we witness a tragedy on our TV screen.

Perhaps we have a strong desire to hold on to some special feeling or experience, yet deep down we know that this is as futile as pretending that a snapshot can be the reality of every morning after.

Some never recognize the ache for what it is. The reason for this ache, in the words of one writer, is that 'in the middle of life we are in death'. We want to achieve, to possess so much. A capacity for life seems at times without limit. Yet we know deep down that nothing will last. It will all fade away.

> **Our days are like grass.**
> **We flourish like a flower of the field.**
> **The wind passes over it and it is gone,**
> **and its place knows it no more.**
> PSALM 103:15,16

That is the ache. The ache is there as a 'prompt'. It prompts us to accept our mortality. Only when we accept that we shall lose it all will we be free to live fully, not as a right, but as a gift.

MAKE DEATH YOUR *ANAM CARA*

In 1997 John O'Donohue wrote a book entitled *Anam Cara* which became a bestseller. *Anam cara* is the Gaelic for 'soul friend'. The soul friend of his book is not a person, it is death. O'Donohue writes:

> Death is the great wound in the universe, the root of all fear and negativity. Friendship with our death would enable us to celebrate the eternity of the soul which death cannot touch...[1]

Continually to transfigure the faces of your own death ensures that at the end of your life your physical death will be no stranger, robbing you against your will of the life that you have had. You will know its face intimately. Since you have overcome your fear, your death will be a meeting with a lifelong friend from the deepest side of your nature.

Death can be understood as the final horizon. Beyond there, the deepest well of your identity awaits you. In that well, you will behold the beauty and light of your eternal face.

Benjamin Franklin understood death in this way:

> A man is not completely born until he is dead ... We are spirits. That bodies should be lent us, while they afford us pleasure, assist us in acquiring knowledge, or in doing good to our fellow creatures, is a kind and benevolent act of God. When they become unfit for these purposes, and afford us pain instead of pleasure, instead of an aid become an encumbrance, and answer none of the intentions for which they were given, it is equally kind and benevolent that a way is provided by which we may get rid of them. Death is that way.[2]

A great nineteenth-century Russian spiritual director, Ivanov Macarios, wrote to a widow:

> I thank you having revealed to me the sadness of your grief-stricken heart; a great radiance comes over me when I share with

others their sorrow. Complete, perfect, detailed compassion is the only answer I can give to your tender love of me that has led you, at such a time, to seek me out in my distant, humble hermitage.[3]

Claire Evans was dying, leaving behind a husband and an 11-year-old son. I recall her saying something like this to me: 'I don't know exactly what is coming next. But throughout my life I have listened to a voice deep inside me, and whenever I have followed this voice I have found that there is a response which makes me believe that the world is, at heart, a friend.'

Practise making a friend of death in every way you can, especially by listening to the voice deep inside you.

'I don't want to think about death,' a 20-year-old friend told me. 'I want to live all out and just go out in a twinkle.'

He thought he had no problem, but so do alcoholics who refuse help. They are in denial. A first step in the Alcoholics Anonymous rehabilitation programme is to recognize that there is a problem. It is like that with death.

Ernest Becker, in his Pulitzer prize-winning book *Denial of Death*, asserts that the reality of our mortality constitutes the fundamental human terror, and our effort to come to terms with it 'is a mainspring of human activity – activity designed largely to avoid the fatality of death, to overcome it by denying in some way that it is the final destiny of man'. In other words, if we don't face this when we are young, we may spend the rest of our lives handcuffed to death rather than being truly free to be ourselves.

Another reason to start preparing for a good death when we are young is that we may die young. Millions of young people are killed through war, accident or illness each year.

WHY DO PEOPLE DIE YOUNG?

It is not a bad idea to start thinking about this: it begins to familiarize us with death. Here are some answers people give to this question:

- Good and evil happenings affect the whole human family, like the sun and the rain, without distinction.
- God wants a variety of people in heaven, so young as well as aged mortals need to enter it.
- In the words of a dying boy to his mother, 'Don't worry, Mum, my body's only my reflection.'

A further reason for starting to prepare for death when we are young is that old habits die hard, but habits learned early come in handy later.

I met a couple who were dynamic leaders of a tough youth centre. They decided on a job change, and were shortly to become wardens of an old people's home. I asked them why they were making such an unlikely change. 'We have realized,' they told me, 'that in old age the negative habits that people display in youth come to the surface again. In the working years in between they have merely been covered up. We ourselves will be like those negative young people when we are aged, unless we work on it now. That is what we will now do.'

Good Pope John XXIII started to prepare for his death when he was a student. He used to play a kind of game, imagining that he was on his deathbed. Years later, he made a wonderful death which inspired the world.

You may, of course, be past youth or middle age. There is still hope. Research into the effects of smoking reveals that, although the highest health ratings go to those who gave up smoking from their youth, there is still a measurable improvement in health if lifelong smokers give up the habit as soon as they realize they have a life-threatening condition. It is like that with our preparations for our final goodbye.

PICTURE DEATH

Artists through the ages have tried to portray death. The artist Paul Klee died relatively young, and *Death and Fire* is one of his last works. A great dome of sun is held aloft by the skull of Death. Art critic Sister Wendy Becket comments:

> The man who approaches is stripped to his essence: Is he humanity moving towards the grave? All this might seem sombre, yet the painting is aglow with the most life-affirming colour ... Klee announces that death is a purifier, like fire, and a means of fulfilment.[4]

The artist Rex Whistler, who was killed in World War II, wrote this:

> I suppose it is really the exquisite taste and economy of the Genius who draws our lives which makes life so infinitely lovely and moving, stirring and glorious. It is as though we presumed to stand by the side of a great painter imploring him not to use the dark tones and shadows, but only to put light and more light. How can we know what the great mind has conceived the finished work to be?[5]

The Jewish Talmud also sees a link between embracing death and discovering blessed fire:

> When Adam saw for the first time the sun go down and an ever deepening gloom enfold creation, his mind was filled with terror. God then took pity on him, and endowed him with the divine intuition to take two stones – the name of one was 'Darkness' and the name of the other 'Shadow of Death' – and rub them against each other, and so discover fire. Thereupon Adam exclaimed with grateful joy: 'Blessed be the Creator of light!'

Fire burns surface material and rubbish, but it purifies really precious things such as gold. If, before I die, I dispense with the flotsam, and let gold develop within me, I need not fear.

MASTER THE FEAR OF DEATH

The primal fear of extinction haunts us. Yet, as Franklin D. Roosevelt said, 'The only thing we have to fear is fear itself.'

A man comes to learn from a Japanese swordsmaster, who tells him, 'You already seem to be a master.'

'The only thing I have mastered is the fear of death,' the man replies.

'Then you are already a master,' the swordsmaster says.

The Japanese arts recognize that you have to meet the fear of death in order to do anything – landscape painting, flower arranging, and so on. If you take the fear of humiliation, or of exposing yourself, and you ask what is frightening about that and try to trace it, you realize that you have a whole series of linkages in your mind which ultimately go back to the fear of death. That is actually the stuff that is controlling you, and if you were not connected up to all that, you would not be afraid to do anything.

The fear of death takes many different disguises. That is why I say it has to be faced over and over again by every society and by every individual.[6]

THE FACES OF DEATH

The faces of death leer at us through life. The face of **fear** may lurk in the background, and then suddenly loom large. It is likely to do this when we face the unknown, danger, pain, loss of security or mobility, and ultimately extinction. Such fear mars our lives. D.H. Lawrence wrote, 'The English ... are paralysed by fear ... That is what thwarts and distorts the Anglo-Saxon existence ... Shakespeare is morbid with fear, fear of consequences.'

This condition is not limited to the English, of course. What is the answer? If we name the fear and bring it out into the light of day, it recedes. So name the fear, then drag it into the centre of an imaginary circle of love. 'Perfect love casts out fear,' writes Saint John. Watch it diminish. Only by journeying to the places of greatest fear will we discover the source of strength that is stronger even than death.

Another face of death is **loneliness**. This is not the same as solitude, which contains no loss of wellbeing. Some cope by clinging to a person, place or project, but all these will come to an end. Where will we be then?

Others disguise this inner loneliness by whizzing around, getting hooked on virtual reality, or by being glued to chat sites on the web. All these will come to an end. Where will we be then?

Only by journeying into the place of greatest loneliness will we rise above a life of subterfuges. Bring your loneliness into that same circle of love.

A third face of death is **anger** due to loss of ego control. Abusive, pushy or defensive behaviour is a sign of this. Racism is another sign. Some cope by forming addictive habits, or by making success their god. But these things have feet of clay. When these crumble, where will we be?

Only by journeying into the place of loss of control can we find lasting freedom.

There are other faces of death, such as **despair** and **pretence**. These, too, if they are to lose their hold over us, have to be named, owned and brought into the circle of love.

SEE ETERNITY IN A GRAIN OF SAND

One way to befriend death when we are young is to see in the things that are visible intimations of things that are invisible. We need to take time out to do this.

> To the north the mountain ranges stood like kings upon their thrones. The sky was an arch of pearl. A cloud city, with towers and battlements complete, went floating by. The mystery of the Infinite was about us. Then the old stalker spoke. 'Is it not fine,' he mused, 'to be abroad on a day like this? For, look you, the high places win the heart to peace, and here a man gazes on the mirror of his own eternity.' ALISTAIR MACLEAN, *Hebridean Altars*[7]

> To see a world in a grain of sand,
> And heaven in a wild flower,
> Hold infinity in the palm of your hand,
> And eternity in an hour.
> WILLIAM BLAKE, *Auguries of Innocence*

This approach has been made famous by William Wordsworth's ode 'Intimations of Immortality', which ends with these words:

> To me the meanest flower that blows can give
> Thoughts that do often lie too deep for tears.

These intimations often came to Wordsworth as he 'wandered lonely as a cloud' among 'a host of golden daffodils'. They led him to conclude, in the words of his ode:

> Our noisy years seem moments in the being
> Of the eternal silence.

RAINBOWS

Our hearts do indeed leap up when we behold a rainbow in the sky, yet it disappears as suddenly as it appears. The rainbow seems to say to us, 'This life is ephemeral, but there is something that lies beyond it.'

HARBOURS AND HORIZONS

Little fishing boats securely tucked up in the safety of a harbour after the ups and downs of their days at sea speak to us of homecoming, and of the final harbour of this life. When we are young it is good to enter wholeheartedly into both the choppy seas and the homecomings of life.

Human beings are touched by the mystery of horizons. As a boat disappears from our own horizon, it may appear on the horizon of people on the other side of the sea. Is it like that with our dying?

BIRDS AND WINDS

Birds and winds come and go, and often we do not know where they come from or where they are going. It is amazing that birds can travel over 3,000 miles from a place, and return to that exact place three years later without map or compass.

The sensation of flying often comes into our dreams. Like the birds, there seems some mysterious instinct in us which calls us to transcend our present limitations. Is this an intimation of immortality?

NATURE'S CYCLE OF REBIRTH

Flowers blooming and fading, the sun rising and setting, animals hibernating and mating – the cycle of dying and rebirth is all around us. Is it not also within us?

When you are bursting with life in the pleasure of bright sunshine, say a prayer like the following, in order to connect your now with your end:

> As the sun above pours its love on my body,
> So at the hour of my death
> Pour your grace on my soul.

Find something that you can place in the palm of your hand and gaze at. Keep gazing until you become aware of the mystery to which this points.

LIVE LIFE AS A JOURNEY

It is not possible to die well if we see life as our unchanging posses-
sion and death as its thief.

> What then are you, human life?
>
> You are the road to life, not life itself.
> You are a real road but not a level one.
> Long for some, short for others,
> Broad for some, narrow for others,
> Joyful for some, sad for others,
> For all alike, fleeting and irrevocable.
> A road is what you are, a road,
> But you are not clear to all.
> Many see you
> And few understand you to be a road.
> For you are so wily and enticing
> That few know you are a road.
>
> Therefore you are to be questioned
> But not believed and given bail.
> You are to be traversed but not inhabited...
>
> For no one dwells on a road, but travels it
> So that those who walk upon the road
> May dwell in their homeland.
>
> COLUMBANUS[8]
>
> I have done my best in the race of life,
> I have run the full distance...
> Now the prize of victory awaits me.
>
> PAUL OF TARSUS

START WITH LIFE'S LITTLE DEATHS

> We ourselves, in some cases, prudently choose a partial death. A mangled, painful limb which cannot be restored we willingly cut off. He who plucks out a tooth parts with it freely, since then pain goes with it. And he who quits the whole body parts at once with all pains and possibilities of pains and diseases which it was liable to. BENJAMIN FRANKLIN

Our last day on earth is best thought of as our final, rather than as our only death. There are lots of 'little deaths' before that. In one sense, this is good news. It gives us a chance to practise going through little deaths without fear and even with flair.

We encounter little deaths whenever we experience loss. The philosopher Friedrich Nietzsche pointed out that, 'The dying person has probably lost during the course of life things more important than what they are about to lose by dying.'

We can experience loss of all the following:

- A friendship
- An ambition
- A job
- A home
- A bodily part
- Good looks
- Self-esteem
- Reputation
- Security

The way we handle loss often proves to be more important than the fact of loss in itself. Out of every defeat a victory can be snatched.

My train or car breaks down. This thwarts my strong desire to be present at an event that is important to me. My instinct is to be angry, to become tense, and not to be present to myself or to those around me. I have a choice, however. I can choose to say, 'God, I place into your hands the situation I was bound for ... Now I place into your hands the situation I find myself in.' Whenever our ego wants its own way and we allow it to 'die', we are, gently and gradually, preparing for our final death.

Why not think through some current or possible little deaths of which you are conscious? Practise embracing loss, and using it as a foundation for building something deeper and more lasting.

PRACTISE GOING TO SLEEP

Every time we go to sleep it is a little death, for we sink into unconsciousness and lose control of our life.

> A dying person needs to die as a sleepy person needs to sleep.
> There comes a time when it is wrong, as well as useless, to resist.
> NEWSPAPER COLUMNIST STEWART ALSOP, D. 1974

Christians and others often think of sleep as a nightly foretaste of death. Therefore, as we practise laying down in rest, we also practise laying down our lives in our final rest.

To sleep requires us to let go of things that preoccupy us and to trust ourselves to the unknown, to the dark, to the possibility of a new dawn following a period of unconsciousness.

Breathe deeply. Relax. As you breathe out, let all that is past ebb away. Then breathe in the sweet, renewing grace of sleep.

This is an instinctive act of trust. This small amount of trust can grow into the greater trust needed for the last time we sleep on earth.

The following is a good prayer to repeat before sleep:

> Sleep, sleep, and away with sorrow,
> Sleep in the arms of Jesus.
> Sleep in the calm of all calm,
> Sleep in the love of all loves.
> Sleep in the lap of the Lord of life.

PRACTISE MAKING TRANSITIONS

At the point of death we have to relinquish control of our body, our brain, our timetable, our relationships, our programme – of everything. This is very difficult for some of us. If we are not used to doing this in lesser ways, it can create enormous tension, unhappiness and even violent death throes.

It makes sense to practise making transitions now. Nature provides examples of creatures who make transitions which can encourage us. The plant-eating tadpole makes the gradual transition into an insect-eating toad. The water creature loses its gills and gains lungs which enable the toad to breathe air. The intestines shorten and legs grow.

Scientists tell us that we humans shed and replace all our skin every seven years. At death our skin shrinks because a different part of us is replaced – the non-material part of us.

Make a space at least once a week to become aware of what or who you are holding on to. Write this down on a piece of paper, and then burn this or throw it away, to symbolize that you are relinquishing control of this bit of your life.

What follows? Often it is greater freedom, peace or clarity.

The next week, go on to some other area of your life where you need to relinquish control. As you do this, you realize that you gain more than you lose when you make these transitions, and so trust grows within you that all will be well when you make the last transition of all.

PRACTISE BEING ON
YOUR DEATHBED

Some traditions think that the sequenced loss of physical powers during the dying process mirrors in reverse the vulnerable struggles towards life of the birth process. The dissolution of the physical organs is sometimes likened to the different elements of earth, water, fire and air. Human beings are encouraged to simulate the dying process while they are in good health. Let us do this now, using the analogy of the elements.

1. EARTH AND THE DISSOLUTION OF THE BODY

I weaken until I have no strength or control over my body. I have to let go of bodily elements – muscle, sex, eyes, mouth. I know that I am made from the elements of the earth and am dissolving back into earth. I need to go with the flow.

2. WATER AND LOSS OF CONTROL OF BODILY FLUIDS

In my mother's womb I was floating in liquid and had no control over this. Now, once again, it is like that. Perhaps I dribble or am incontinent, yet my eyes are so dry. I need to go with the flow.

3. FIRE AND THE DRYING UP OF BODILY PARTS

Not only my eyes now, but also my mouth and nose are dried up. My brain also seems to sink. Memories blur. Maybe I cannot recognize loved ones. Maybe I call out to my mother, not realizing that she left this earth long ago. It feels like being in the middle of a fire. I am being consumed. I need to allow this to happen.

4. AIR AND THE DISSOLUTION OF CONSCIOUSNESS

It is harder to breathe, to think. The gap between this life and the next is now very thin. I rasp and pant. My intellect disintegrates. Everything is a blur. I hallucinate. I may be terrified, or, if I am close to God, I may see saints, angels or beautiful scenes.

Now the physical elements are dissolving into 'trans-body' consciousness. Breathing ceases. I am declared 'dead'.

PRACTISE PRAYING

Sometimes, during a holiday or a free day, it is good to walk in a quiet place or along a cemetery path and recite prayers that will help you along your final journey on earth. If they become part of you now, they will be a strength to you then.

Alistair Maclean, in his book *Hebridean Altars*, recalls how the Hebridean islanders used to go singing through the valley:

> When Thou shalt close this mouth of mine,
> Mine heart lose power to sob,
> When my breath shall cease to rattle,
> When my pain shall cease to throb,
> Then relieve me, and receive me,
> And conduct my soul to God.[9]

He records three other prayers of Hebridean islanders, the first that of an old farmer on the island of Coll.

> Be with me and for me, dear Lord,
> as I walk upon the road of brightness
> that runs between earth and Thy glory.

> Saviour and Friend, how wonderful art Thou,
> My companion upon the changeful way,
> The comforter of its weariness,
> My guide to the Eternal Town,
> The welcome at its gate.

> O Holy Christ, bless me with your presence when my days are drear.
> Bless me with your presence when my joy is full.
> Bless me with your presence when I reach my end.
> Help me in the darkness to find the ford.

Why not make up your own prayers on these themes? Michael Halliwell, from Jersey, wrote this prayer:

Lord of the sunrise, source and ground of my being,
you know me in my mother's womb.
As my first day begins, heal me of the pain and hurt I receive.

Lord of the dawn, you see me grow strong as I learn to walk and talk,
heal me of tears of separation and loss.

Lord of the high noon, you accompany me along life's journey,
guide me in choice and strengthen me in adversity.

Lord of the dusk, as my life declines,
help me to surrender all that I have and all that I am into your hand.

Lord of the sunset, as I go to my eternal home,
strengthen me on my last journey with you,
that I may entrust my soul into your hands in faith and hope.

GET TO KNOW YOUR BODY

Not one cell of our bodies is built to last for ever. We are designed to grow out of each stage of our life on earth. Being born, growing up, maturing, ageing and dying are all part of a natural process. If we co-operate with this process throughout our lives, we are more likely to co-operate with it at our end.

Cosmetic surgery can disguise or delay our ageing for a short time only. Deep-freezing our bodies at or near death merely delays the inevitable, and stores up future discontinuities.

We co-operate when we accept what is happening to our bodies: we can no longer play football; the menopause arrives; wrinkles appear; hairs go grey; teeth fall out; we need others to assist us.

To co-operate also means that we stop pretending to be what we are not. Why pretend to be a spring chicken if we are in fact a golden oldie? We can still aim to be our best. If we are an oldie, we can aim to be a glorious golden oldie. We can aim to grow old gracefully.

MOVE WITH LIFE'S RHYTHMS

Full tide, ebb tide
Let life's rhythms flow
Ebb tide, full tide
How life's beat must go.

DAVID ADAM[10]

The ebb tide might be a setback or a disappointment. It might be a low biorhythm or a seasonal disorder. It might be exhaustion or depression after a prolonged period of activity.

By learning to go with the ebb tide, we learn also to go with the incoming tide. There is a time to rest and a time to act. If we fail to practise this rhythm, we fail to become renewed. We become like an overused machine which is fit only for the scrapheap.

Go with the ebb tide and, if the tide comes in again, think that you have prepared yourself for the final ebb time.

We also need to learn to flow with the seasons. We cannot enjoy the autumn if we won't let go of summer. We can't experience new life in spring if we have lived through winter at summer's pace. By learning to go with the rhythm of the seasons, we embrace the cycle of death and rebirth. These cycles reflect in an earthly way a truth about the world of the spirit. If we embrace this, we also embrace death as a friend.

Let go of summer

The leaves are falling gently
In their colours of yellow and brown
Hanging on to the last
Before finally falling down.

Each letter to the earth
Is posted by the wind
For nature knows just what to keep
And what she should rescind.

Though we like to cling to warmth
And the joy of longer days
We need to restock our strength
In store for winter's ways.

Let us write our own farewell
As the fading summer goes
Seeking a different vision
In the way that nature shows.

STEVE FRANKLIN PALMER[II]

COME THROUGH ROUGH PASSAGES

Although some of us have sweet and untroubled deaths, we need to face the fact that for others dying will be a rough passage.

These things can be rough:

- Constricted breathing
- Accumulating fluids
- Terror
- Excruciating pain
- Loneliness
- Loss of control
- The death rattle

Some cry out to end it all, and a few do just that.

There is another way to approach this, however: to gain experience of coming through rough passages in life, and so also in death.

A rough passage in life might consist of any of these things:

- An illness
- A broken relationship
- An unjust situation
- Breakdown
- Debt
- Failure

Always remember that the journey is as important as the destination. How we handle defeat is more important than what we have lost. Qualities of perseverance, humility and unselfishness can only grow if we have arenas in which to exercise them.

Practise being fully present to another during a rough moment today. Hang on in there. Make it your aim to exit this life as an overcomer; to go out in triumph, not defeat.

RED, WHITE AND BLUE DEATHS

Three kinds of death were once sought after in a popular movement. These were red, white and blue deaths.

Red was the colour of the martyrs, people of great spirit who allowed their blood to be shed rather than deny what they knew to be right and true. Stories of their noble deaths during the early centuries of the persecution of Christians stirred many people to rededicate their lives.

When the period of persecution passed, these rededicated people asked themselves, 'Is it possible to be a martyr in a different way?' They may have read what Jerome wrote to a young woman whose widowed mother had given away all her possessions and entered a convent:

> Your mother has been crowned because of her long martyrdom. It is not only the shedding of blood which is the mark of a true witness, but the service of a dedicated heart is a daily martyrdom. The first is wreathed with a crown of roses and violets, the second of lilies.

They also read in *The Life of St Martin*, the first person to be officially declared a saint who had not been killed for his faith:

> He achieved martyrdom without blood. For of what human sorrows did he not, for the hope of eternity, endure the pain – in hunger, in night watchings ... in the persecutions of the wicked, in care for the sick, in anxiety for those in peril.[12]

They therefore decided to call those who gave up home and possessions in order to serve God and others 'white martyrs'.

The Irish came up with a third idea, that of 'blue martyrs' (blue being the colour of death), linked to extended penance or pilgrimage, going into exile from home comforts for the love of God.

The twentieth century had more red martyrs than any other century. Perhaps the twenty-first century will have more white and blue martyrs than any previous century? We can each be a martyr by laying aside everything that comes between us and God, or by laying down our life for our neighbour.

It is certain that, as we practise laying down our lives in any form, we shall be better able to lay them down at the curtain call.

REACH FOR THE EDGES

A good way to befriend the ultimate edge of life is to reach for the edges in various aspects of life. These may be physical, moral or spiritual edges.

David Blaine, 25, buried himself alive in a plastic coffin for a week. He did this after experiencing his mother's funeral. A year later, wearing nothing but combat trousers, boots and a woollen hat, he agreed to be entombed for two days in a six-ton block of ice. 'I enjoy setting myself goals,' he explained. 'This is my way of challenging every human fear.'[13]

That may be bizarre, but it is good to challenge our fears.

Kevin, at roughly the same age as David, went to live in a tomb cut out of the rock 50 feet above a lough. His clothes were animal skins. Each day he prayed for an hour in the icy waters, even when a scaly sea creature, feared by local fishermen, curled itself around him. Kevin of Glendalough had discovered this truth: 'Go to the place of your greatest fear and it will become the place of your greatest strength.'

The exploits of David and Kevin are not for everyone. Indeed, some would regard them as foolhardy, just as they would the exploits of bungee-jumpers and paragliders.

There are other ways of reaching for the edge. Howard was president of his student union, and an atheist. Some Christians challenged him to make an experiment: to do unconditionally whatever his conscience told him to do. The results were so startling that Howard, a scientist, concluded the most likely explanation was that there was an unseen, superior Intelligence. He followed his conscience to the edge, and in time became a believer in God.

Nobody can reach to the edge of life itself until their time comes to die. Nonetheless, if we have learned to reach for other edges in our lives, we will surely be more able to reach for the final edge.

REVIEW YOUR LIFE

I mentioned earlier that Good Pope John XXIII practised imagining he was on his deathbed from his student days. This stood him in good stead. When he was dying of a painful cancer, he refused medication in order to be fully present to the world and to God.

I try to review my life at least once a year. The froth recedes. Important things which have been left undone come to my notice, and I still have time to do something about them.

Here is a way to review your life which was passed on to me. You might want to record or write these things down. Take plenty of time and come back to some of the points if you need to.

* * *

I imagine that today I am to die. I ask for time to be alone, and write down for my friends a sort of testimony.

1 **These things in life I have**
   loved:

   tasted:

   looked at:

smelled:

heard:

touched:

2 These experiences I have cherished:

3 These persons are enshrined within my heart:

4 These convictions I have lived by:

5 These are the things I have lived for:

6 These insights I have gained in the school of life:

7 These risks I took:

8 These sufferings have matured me:

9 These lessons life has taught me:

10 My life has been shaped by these
    persons:

occupations:

books:

events:

11 These things I regret about my life:

12 These are my unfulfilled desires:

13 These are my life's achievements:

I choose an end to this document – a poem (my own or someone else's), a prayer, a sketch, a picture from a magazine, a Scripture text, or anything else that I judge would be an apt conclusion to my testament. I place or write below the points I have made.

BE PRESENT TO THE DYING

By being present to a loved one who is dying, we are making ourselves familiar with a journey that we, too, will one day make. Sometimes relatives or friends refuse to accept that their loved one is dying, so they don't talk about it. This means that the dying person is denied the chance to share what they are really feeling. It is a terrible letdown.

We should not tell a dying person what they do not wish to be told, but we can draw out from them what they are feeling, we can recall past experiences, and we can thank them for their friendship.

Farewells can be said in ways other than words. We can hold someone's hand, stroke their brow, or even ask to wash their body. It is important to be comfortable. For some people, singing old favourites helps to relax them and reminds them of being sung to as a child.

What if you can't be there at the time of the death or the funeral? You could do any of these things:

- Light a candle.
- Look at a photo and cry or talk to the one you love.
- Write a message on a card.
- Recall stories.
- Say your own prayers.

Some people treat Jesus as a mediator between the person who remains on earth and their loved one who has died. They pour out everything to Jesus and ask him to communicate to the deceased whatever is best for them.

Say goodbye in good time. If possible, don't leave it until the power of speech or thought recedes. This allows us to be beside loved ones, enjoying the satisfaction of having said what is in our hearts for them. Is this not what we will one day wish for ourselves from others?

ENJOY THE COMMUNION OF SAINTS

No consolation can be so certain and so lasting to you as that softened and manly sorrow which springs up from the memory of the Dead. CHARLES DICKENS

Many questions arise when someone we are close to dies. Are their souls conscious? Do they remember us? Are they still involved in some way in our lives? C.S. Lewis wrote this to a friend whose father had died:

> I feel very strongly (and I am not alone in this) that some good comes from the dead to the living in the months or weeks after the death. I think I was much helped by my own father after his death; as if our Lord welcomed the newly dead with the gift of some power to bless those they have left behind ... Certainly they often seem just at that time to be very near us.[14]

Many religions believe that there are bodiless as well as embodied spirits. Christianity believes in this, and in what it calls 'the communion of saints'. However, churches in the West from the fourteenth century onwards got in a tangle about how we should relate to holy souls who have died. Catholics added on what their critics thought were superstitious ideas. Protestants, according to their critics, threw out the baby as well as the bathwater by making the role of the dead a no-go area.

Before Christianity divided into these conflicting traditions (and still today in Orthodox, and increasingly again in new Western churches), 'the communion of saints' was understood as follows.

Christ is truly divine, truly human, ever living, and the Head of his Body, which is the Church on earth and in heaven – all who have ever been joined to him. All who are joined to Christ have his life and his mind flowing through them. So the Church on earth carries in its prayers the whole Church, on earth and in heaven. And the Church in heaven, like its Head, carries in its heart the whole Church, on earth as well as in heaven, although each does this according to their particular calling.

The Bible indicates that believers who have died are alert and aware, even though they have not yet received what the Bible calls their 'resurrection body'. For example, in relation to great believers such as Abraham, Jesus says about God, 'He is not the God of the dead but of the living' (Luke 20:38). Hebrews 12:22–4 says that we mortals are in the presence, not only of God and of angels, but also of just souls who have been made perfect. It would surely not say this if they were inactive and unaware. Paul was sure he would be alive after his death, saying he desired 'to depart and be with Christ' (Philippians 1:23, NRSV). Although, from the point of view of those of us who remain on earth, those who have died are 'asleep', this is only a temporary, physical separation.

From the time of Jesus, when the prophets Elijah and Moses appeared to him and three friends on a mountain (see Matthew 17:1–8), and throughout Christian history, certain Christ-like persons have appeared to people living on earth. This is unsolicited, a divine gift, and should not be confused with the practice of summoning up the dead, which is forbidden in the Bible (see Leviticus 19:31; 20:6).

The Church, knowing all this, found nothing in the Scriptures that would prohibit Christians from expressing a sense of fellowship with those who have died.

One way to do this is to visualize the communion of saints in sign, singing and sacrament. Perhaps the most natural way to do it is to pray for them – not to change their state of salvation (for their eternal destiny is already decided by God, as Hebrews 9:27 tells us), but rather to share in the process which never ends, of 'being changed from glory into glory' (2 Corinthians 3:18).

Those who ask the saints to pray for them are asking them to help them by praying to God. Since God alone is Uncreated, and we are created beings, we should not imagine that there is no variety of responsibility or closeness to God in heaven.

Even if you are among those Christians who do not believe your prayers can affect those in heaven, you can still talk to God about those who have died, simply because it helps to do so. Since Jesus is the Mediator between God and humans (see 1 Timothy 2:5), we can pour out everything we want to say to our departed loved ones and ask Jesus to communicate to them anything of this that he thinks is appropriate. Thus our prayers for the departed can help to preserve and increase the unity between the Church on earth and the Church in heaven.

In many parts of the world, suffering people have been upheld through their belief that a saintly Christian who gave their life for that area is still interceding to God for them in their time of need. Sometimes, in a crisis, there have been visions of the saint followed by a miracle. In Georgia, Southern Russia, Christians often sing a hymn to St Nina, who brought the Faith to that country, which concludes, 'With the angels you have praised in song the Redeemer, praying constantly for us that Christ may grant us His grace and mercy.' Many people in northern England strongly sensed that Durham City and Cathedral were saved during World War II by the prayers of St Cuthbert, who is buried there.

Christians believe that death cannot sever the bond of mutual love between the members of the Church on earth and in heaven.

For all the saints who from their labours rest,
Who Thee by faith before the world confessed,
Thy name, O Jesu, be for ever blest,
Alleluia!

O blest communion, fellowship divine!
We feebly struggle, they in glory shine.
Yet all are one in Thee, for all are Thine.
Alleluia!

W. WALSHAM HOW, 1823–97

ENCOUNTER ANGELS

As I write this, angels are sweeping the worlds of pop songs, book-shops and conferences. According to tradition, one of the angels' big jobs is to help young people make friends of death. But this involves a challenge, which I thought of when I had to speak in Los Angeles (the City of Angels) on the day their Christmas decorations went up. Every street glittered with brilliant Hollywood-style Christmas figures, including angels.

I issued this challenge: 'My subject is "How to Prepare a Celtic Christmas". Since almost nothing is known about Celtic Christmases, I can't give you a shopping list of things to get. I can simply point out two ways you can approach Christmas. The first way is to spend time and money putting up the world's best angel figures, such as you see around you. The second way is so to live that you can actually encounter an angel for real, as did Mary, Joseph and the shepherds at Jesus' birth. In order to do this, you have to let go of the world of glitter and enter into stillness...'

I know people who have seen an angel. In fact, according to Hope MacDonald, who saw an angel with her husband which saved them from getting a divorce, one in six people she questioned had seen or felt an angel presence. It is never too early to develop sensitivity to the unseen world.

Become still. Become aware of the presences around you, within you. Hold imaginary conversations with your guardian angel, the angel who will one day escort you into the worlds beyond this.

TRANSFORMATIONS

When the earth shall claim your limbs, then shall you truly dance. KAHLIL GIBRAN[15]

Is anything more beautiful than the transformation of a chrysalis into a butterfly? Some people believe that there is one thing more beautiful even than that: the transformation of a human from an earth creature into a being no longer bound by earth.

A human wreck brought into one of Mother Teresa's homes said, 'I will have lived the life of a beast, and I shall die like an angel.'

Marie de Hennezel, in her book *Intimate Death*, tells of her visit to a 25-year-old drug addict on the day she announced she was going to die of cancer. Abandoned at birth by her prostitute mother, the addict had lived a hard, loveless life, ceasing at nothing to slake her wild thirst for love.

When Marie arrived, the patient deliberately pulled from her face the oxygen tubes which kept her breathing. She moved into the position women adopt for childbirth. Then she pushed down her legs as if she were giving birth.

Spellbound, Marie stroked her, and knew intuitively that she must not replace the oxygen tubes. Into her mind came Michael de M'Uzan's words about the spiritual labour that goes on inside every dying person – 'an effort to give birth to oneself completely before leaving'. This young woman, who had been pushed to the edge of life, was birthing herself into a new world.[16]

It is not only at the end of life, or in the mythic wizard world of Harry Potter, that transformations take place. They can take place during our journey through life. We can practise discarding things that have had their day, and being birthed into something new.

Is there a transformation waiting to happen in your life? By allowing something new to come into being now, you will be better able to allow something new to come into being at the end of the journey.

BE PREPARED!

The only motto I can remember from my childhood is the one taught me by the Boy Scouts: 'Be prepared.' In order to get my award for a camping trek, I had to satisfy the examiners that I had prepared for all sorts of exigencies. How do you pitch your tent when the ground is frozen? How do you find the right route when the wind blows the instructions from your hand? How do you light a fire to cook a meal if the matches are too sodden?

If the examiners had paid a lightning visit during those hours of emergency, would they have declared me ready to tackle the next award project?

Jesus told a story about the owner of an enterprise who entrusted its management to various people. When the owner paid a surprise visit, he found them asleep and the project in a shambles. Jesus' point was that God is like the owner, and might call us from our earth responsibilities at any time.

This reminds me of another Boy Scout saying: 'The rent we pay for being allowed to live on earth is to be useful.'

We need always to be on our toes, so that if death suddenly takes us, we are ready in our spirits, doing what we are meant to be doing at that moment, and ready for whatever lies in store for us next.

PART TWO
***
GROW BEFORE YOU GO

Gather together the fragments of your lives
make good endings
Do not pine away ...
Seek to live from the depths of your wounds
Accumulate timeless treasure.

LIVE SIMPLY

My aged friend Neville was resigned to dying, but he was not ready to die well. Fortunately for him, the first time he seemed at death's door he had a dream which presaged a recovery. This gave him another opportunity to get into a right state to die.

He dreamed he was in a large airport departure lounge. He began walking out to the runway with his pile of black suitcases, but the cases proved to be too heavy. He had to wheel them back into the airport lounge and unpack them. There was one suitcase inside another, each slightly smaller. Eventually, when the suitcases were all unpacked, he left them behind in the departure lounge, and walked nobly to the runway with nothing but a leotard.

It is good to depart life in the beauty of simplicity. We can take nothing with us, and there is nothing worse, either for ourselves or for our loved ones, than to leave behind a mess. The time to learn simplicity is now.

Jesus advises us to be like someone who has to look after a house for the owner. We must be ready for the owner to summon us at any time to give an account (see Matthew 24:44–6).

Here are three things to help us live like this:

1 Get rid of clutter and things we do not need.
2 Make a will.
3 Keep in one place, in a tidy form, all the information our next of kin would need if we suddenly died.

This is a way of being unselfish, so that we do not leave an unnecessary burden for someone else to carry.

DO IT NOW!

Both my parents got inoperable cancer at about the age of 57. At that same age I had an inexplicable and continuing stomach pain. The night before I went to the doctor, I could not sleep. The future looked like a dark, downward-sloping tunnel. I was ready to go through the tunnel, but I suddenly realized how much I relished the gift of life.

How wonderful life is, I thought – and we have only one life to live. There were places I would never now go to, and things I would never now do. I asked myself, 'On my deathbed, what bit of life will I most regret never having savoured? What place will I most regret never having visited? What thing will I most regret never having done?'

There would not be time for much, but if I acted quickly there would be time to see, savour or do the most important thing I had missed out on so far. I thought about various things, such as swimming with dolphins, then I decided what was priority number one: I would go to Venice. 'It would be a crime to have lived on Planet Earth without seeing that jewel of civilization,' I told myself.

The doctor told me I had pulled a stomach muscle in the gym. I was as fit as a fiddle.

I nearly didn't go to Venice – until I remembered the advice I planned to give in this very book: *Do something now about the things you will regret not having done when you are on your deathbed. Choose your first priority. Do it now!*

Venice was wonderful.

What is your 'Venice'? Write down your priority here:

FULFIL YOUR DESTINY

It is possible to die without having lived. Some people who are discharged this life in a coffin have merely existed. Why not fulfil your unique destiny? No one else in the world has fingerprints the same as yours.

It is true that life may have dealt us cruel blows; we may have blown this or that possibility. But God starts where we are.

I believe that God has a Divine Plan for me.

I believe that this plan is wrapped in the folds of my being, even as the oak is wrapped in the acorn and the rose is wrapped in the bud.

I believe that this Plan is permanent, indestructible and perfect, free from all that is essentially bad.

Whatever comes into my life that is negative is not a part of this God-created Plan, but is a distortion caused by my failure to harmonize myself with the Plan as God has made it.

GLENN CLARK[1]

A human life can be like an acorn growing into an oak if we allow the deep places of fear or hurt to be healed. If we don't allow this, we revert at the end of our lives to the spoilt or hurt child that has remained buried in us from childhood.

Even if we have missed plan A, there is always a plan B, which represents the best possibility for us in the present moment. Whatever our outward circumstances, this can be creative and fulfilling.

In order to be fulfilled in our departing, we need first to have lived fully. Although none of us can say, when we die, that we have lived completely whole lives, we can take steps to depart this life more whole and more fulfilled than if we had given no thought to the matter.

Living fully involves reaching for our dreams, using all our senses, flowing in our potential, growing in our relationships.

When I was analysing I observed clearly that the fear of death was in proportion to not-living ... By being alive I mean living out of all the cells, all the parts of oneself. The cells which are denied become atrophied, like a dead arm, and infect the rest of the body. People living deeply have no fear of death. ANAÏS NIN[2]

LISTEN TO YOUR SOUL THOUGHTS

Most of the time we rush too much and do not listen to our deepest thoughts about life and death. The result is that, when we are laid aside, we hardly know our thoughts – and even if we do, we do not know how to put them into words for those we care about.

For the soul to be heard, the mind must be still. Then thoughts and feelings can arise as if from a deep well within us. Illness or frailty can be an opportunity to create spaces when we listen to our soul thoughts.

When we have listened, we should find someone with whom we can share these thoughts – someone with whom we can truly share the depths into which illness, perhaps, is taking us. We need to voice concerns such as these:

- Will our lives have been worthwhile?
- What do we regret doing or not having done?
- What do we still want time for?
- Do we matter?
- Do the people in our lives really matter to us?
- Is there a God?
- Is there an afterlife?
- What unfinished business gnaws at us?
- What long-buried thoughts and memories are coming back to us now?
- What are our dreams saying?

All too often, when we speak of such matters, the impulse of others is to cover up our words hurriedly with a thin layer of reassurance. We respond by withdrawing. Yet what if we were to find a real soul friend, a person to whom we could tell the truth of what we feel, know or perceive?

FACE PAIN

Heroes go through pain barriers. Marathon runners go through 'the wall'. The birth pains of mothers soon give way to joy at the birth of a baby. A lesson of life and of leadership is this: *Do the painful thing first, and you will then have plenty of time to enjoy the rest of what you do. Leave the painful decisions until last, and everything else you do loses its joy.*

Often it is said, 'I do not fear death, but I fear the pain of dying.' A minority of people do go through death agonies, although modern treatments moderate these. Nature has put into our bodies something that automatically numbs pain. This is attested to by people who have been at the point of being burned or crushed, and who survived by some fluke.

We are not given more pain than we can bear. Mystery of meaning is hidden even in pain.

> **Your pain is the breaking of the shell that encloses your understanding.**
>
> **Even as the stone of the fruit must break, that its heart may stand in the sun, so must you know pain.**
>
> **And could you keep your heart in wonder at the daily miracles of your life, your pain would not seem less wondrous than your joy.** KAHLIL GIBRAN[3]

If we face pain throughout our lives, we will surmount it at the end of our lives.

KNOW YOUR LIFE STORY

Some crematoria place a notice by the minister's seat which says, 'Finish the service in 20 minutes – others may be waiting to enter.' A human life is far too wonderful to be dismissed in a standardized 20-minute 'assembly line'.

Often little or nothing that is personal to the deceased is mentioned at a funeral. When it is, however, people often think, 'What a pity that it took a funeral for us to know what sort of person he/she really was.' One thing is even worse: that the deceased valued themselves so little that they themselves did not know the story of their own life. It is only too easy to look upon our life as one cynical historian looked upon history: 'One damn thing after another.'

Part of becoming a whole person is to learn the story of our life. If we belittle or blank out painful episodes, our story can become a mere blur. The good news is that there is a remedy. We can take action to prevent this happening. Routes to major centres have milestones beside the road. We can create milestones for our own life's journey. Some of these milestones might be our memories of such things as love, fun, fear, achievement, discovery, failure or hurt at different stages of life.

* * *

Write down a memory which is a milestone in each of these stages of life:

Baby

Junior

Adolescent

First job

Adult/marriage/partners

Children/family/household

Mid-life

Retirement

Old age

SHARE YOUR LIFE STORY

Country-and-western singer Reba McIntire wrote a song about her father's death and entitled it 'The Greatest Man I Never Knew'. How sad. Yet how many of us experience something similar?

Suppose Reba had worked on a song while her father was still alive? Better still, suppose her father had worked on a song, or even a sentence or two, to share something of himself with her before he died? None of us is meant to leave behind relatives who will describe us, after we are gone, as 'the person I never knew'.

There are always reasons why we do not allow ourselves to be known. These reasons may include shame, fear, shyness, confusion, or an inability to say what we feel. How can we get over these hurdles? Here are some ways.

- Write a letter to a relative and ask someone to give this to them at the right time.
- Make a video of yourself relaxing with friends, family or colleagues in a variety of situations, or record someone interviewing you about yourself.
- Compile a photograph album with captions as a record of your life.
- Record your thoughts on a cassette.
- Write a diary.
- Tell a third party (e.g. a counsellor, priest or family friend) what you really want to say, and leave it to them to communicate this to the person(s) concerned.

LIVE OUT OF YOUR
VULNERABILITY

**Listen to the language of your wounds. Do not pine away in the
pain of them, but seek to live from the depths of them.**
JIM COTTER

Most of the time human beings 'play games'. We 'play the part' that
we think will give us better job or social prospects. We hide behind
façades. We are like an actor playing a role based on someone else's
script.

A castaway who spent a year on the deserted Hebridean island of
Taransay as part of a BBC television social experiment programme
came to this conclusion: 'I used to think that I was what I did and
said. Here I have realized that the real me does not depend upon
what I say and do.' He had realized that, in life outside the island, he
pitched what he said and did to other people's expectations.

Learning to speak and do things that come from our real self
takes courage. Instead of pretending to be strong, we become aware
that we feel weak or fragile. By living this way we risk losing the
approval of others. Yet we become free.

Is it possible that one reason for having to go through the dying
process is that we need to live out of our real, vulnerable self before
we are ready for what lies ahead?

Practise living from your vulnerability now.

You will grow as a person.

You will become free to enter into life.

You will become free to move on from it.

SPEAK OUT YOUR ANGUISH

There comes a time when we each realize it is too late to relive our life, avoiding the hurts, mistakes and neglect that have marred it. Although we cannot go back, we also feel that we cannot go on to our final journey with our anguish still unresolved. We are like a sandwich filling, squeezed between the pain of the past and the future. Conflicting thoughts of grief or anger assault the soul, and threaten to plunge it into despair.

This is the time to speak out all that is within you. A conversation with a friend who was counselling someone in the throes of despair supplied John Bell, the songwriter member of the Iona Community, with the first three verses of the following song, to which the voice of God responds in the last verse.

All the fears I need to name but am too scared to say;
all the shame for what I've done which nothing can allay;
all the people I've let down and lost along the way;
all the hate I still remand.
    Must these torment me to the end of time?
    Who is there to understand?

All the wasted years in which I struggled to be free;
all the broken promises that took their toll on me;
all the love I should have shown and all I failed to be;
all I longed to take my hand.
    Must these torment me to the end of time?
    Who is there to understand?

What the cause of pain is and, much more, the reason why;
what my final hour will bring, how suddenly I'll die;
what the future holds for those I'll miss, for whom I cry;
what, too late, I might demand.
    Shall these torment me to the end of time?
    Who is there to understand?

All the wrong you now admit, I promise to forgive;
all that you regret you are not sentenced to relive;
all the love you've never known is mine alone to give;
you, my child are understood.
  So do not fear all that is yet to be:
  heaven is close and God is good.

JOHN L. BELL[4]

If you cannot find someone to whom you can pour out your anguish, pour it out to God – but, having done that, look for an opportunity to share it with another person.

ENGAGE WITH THE
STAGES OF LIFE

We cannot be joined unless we are first separated. We cannot be viably born until the umbilical cord has been cut. We cannot enter wholeheartedly into adolescence until we break free from our mother's apron strings. We cannot be truly joined to another in marriage unless we first separate, physically and emotionally, from our parents.

The psychologist C.G. Jung thought people went wrong by making youth and young adulthood the ideal for all of life: older people try to copy the young, and consign the second half of life to the rubbish bin. Often this is the cause of the mid-life crisis, and is why some women feel they are finished after the menopause. People often try to deal with this by changing their profession or belief system, or by getting divorced – but repressing one's former life is no answer.

Jung believed that it is necessary to separate from youthfulness in order to enter the second half of life. He also believed that, for the second part of life to be lived to the full, it should be seen as a preparation for death. Shrinking from death robs the second half of life of its significance, for an old person who cannot bid farewell to life is as pathetic as a young person who cannot embrace it.

In the end it is necessary to be separated from the bodily life in order to be joined to the eternal life. By learning to make the appropriate separation at each stage of life, our individuation process progresses, until finally we are able to be joined to the reality that exists after this physical existence has ended.

BE A PILGRIM

Orthodox Christians refer to dying as 'The Great Passage' because it is a move from one stage to another in a person's journey. It makes sense to practise leaving behind one stage of our journey and moving on to another throughout our lives. That is one reason why pilgrim journeys are catching on.

A man from the USA came as a pilgrim to Lindisfarne. He had fainted on the incoming plane, and feared that he might not survive if he had a similar attack on the flight back. He used me as a temporary *Anam Cara*, or soul friend, and began to write his deepest thoughts in a journal.

He invited Jesus to accompany him on the return journey. The day before his departure, he awoke early with stirrings like 'a sunrise of spirit'. He heard the words, 'My pilgrimage is fulfilled,' and described this as 'a lovely pronouncement, touching me with tears of joy'. Next, words from Scripture came to him which connected fainting with death. 'Whether we live or die, we are the Lord's,' was quickly followed by Jesus' words, 'Be not anxious.'

Immediately his fear faded and a quiet trust filled his being. His journey home was good. Pilgrim's progress.

ACCUMULATE TIMELESS TREASURE

I arrived at my gym one day feeling 'the decrepitude of winter'. In contrast to my mood, bright posters smiled at me, offering 'timeless beauty'. 'Can I buy some timeless beauty?' I asked. No. It was only for women, and only for those with good pay packets.

In reality, there is a timeless beauty that every person can acquire. The sooner we acquire it the better. Jesus said, 'Do not store up material treasures that are quickly destroyed, but accumulate time-less treasure that neither moths can eat nor rust can wear away' (Matthew 6:19–20). What did he mean by 'timeless treasure'? His great apostle, Paul, suggested three things that are timeless: faith, hope and love.

In a letter to a friend whose husband had died, the actress Joyce Grenfell wrote:

> We can never lose anything that is good, never lose love or the memories of great happiness because they are *true*. I've come to the conclusion that only the eternal is real!
>
> And that means qualities that one loves in people – their humour, generosity, honour, kindness, gentleness etc. *are* the real-ity: and can never die. They are the identity of the one one loves.[5]

So we build up eternal treasure by developing positive qualities and relationships, by giving our utmost for the highest.

DOES DEATH ROB
LIFE OF ITS MEANING?

Victor Frankl faced death in the ghastly circumstances of a Nazi prison camp, along with many fellow Jews who were exterminated. He survived to become a famous psychotherapist. His fellow prisoners wondered whether death would rob their lives of all meaning. Not so, Victor Frankl told them:

> 'What you have experienced, no power on earth can take from you. Not only our experiences, but all we have done, whatever great thoughts we have had, and all we have suffered, all this is not lost, though it is past; we have brought it into being. Having been is also a kind of being, and perhaps the surest kind.'
>
> Then I spoke of the many opportunities of giving life a meaning. I told my comrades (who lay motionless, although occasionally a sigh could be heard) that human life, under any circumstances, never ceases to have a meaning, and that this infinite meaning of life includes suffering and dying, privation and death. I asked the poor creatures who listened to me attentively in the darkness of the hut to face up to the seriousness of our position. They must not lose hope but should keep their courage in the certainty that the hopelessness of our struggle did not detract from its dignity and its meaning. I said that someone looks down on each of us in difficult hours – a friend, a wife, somebody alive or dead, or a God – and he would not expect us to disappoint him. He would hope to find us suffering proudly – not miserably – knowing how to die.[6]

BECOME FREE TO MOVE ON

To leave some part of our life behind and move on to a new phase requires a degree of confidence. This comes more naturally to some than to others, but it can come to any of us through practice. A few people move on to the completely unknown for the fun of it: thrills and spills give them a fix. Most of us, however, can only trust ourselves to the unknown if we sense that somehow it is a friend.

I took my first ski lessons as a mature adult. Some small children were taking their first lessons at the same time, and they left us oldies standing. Why? Unlike us, they were not afraid to let their bodies go with the skis and with the snow.

'The only thing that can stop you doing that downhill ski is yourself,' I was told. 'Let yourself go.' With great concentration, I abandoned myself to the skiing rather than to my fear. I accomplished the feat.

This taught me a great principle of life and death: *Go with the flow, and you will be free to move on. Fear is the great Stopper.*

The following exercise is a fear-buster.

Conjure up an image that conveys unconditional love. Look into this until your feelings change, until you are drawn towards that unconditional love. Now look behind you. What do you see that you need to leave behind, but fear to do so? Consciously turn your back on what you need to leave behind. Walk away from it towards your image of unconditional love. Let things unfold. What happens?

Now repeat the exercise, imagining you are on your deathbed. You are leaving your whole earthly life behind. Again let things unfold. What happens?

Now move on.

PART THREE

* * *

GO PREPARED

Go well.
Go tidy.
Go having shared.
Go accomplished.
Go free.

WHAT WILL YOU LEAVE BEHIND?

> The life and passion of a person leaves an imprint on the ether of
> a place. Love does not remain within the heart, it flows out to
> build secret tabernacles in a landscape.
>
> JOHN O'DONOHUE, *Anam Cara*

What will you leave behind, apart from possessions, that will enrich
the world after you are gone? It is possible to leave nothing behind.

When Traudl Junge was 22, Hitler chose her to become his fourth
secretary. She stood by him to the end, even accompanying him into
the Berlin bunker. Two hours before he killed himself, Hitler called
her in to write his will. 'I thought I would be the first person to
know why all this had happened. He would say something that
explained it all, that would teach us something, leave us with something,' she said. But in the end, 'It was just the same phrases, in the
same quiet tone, and then, at the end of it, those terrible words
about the Jews. After all the despair, all the suffering, not one word
of sorrow, of compassion. I remember thinking: he has left us with
nothing.'[1]

I would like to leave behind some things I have done, written,
prayed or been that have helped others find wisdom, direction,
friendship or love. I would like to leave behind a spirituality that
offers people a path to fullness of life in God.

What things would you like to leave behind? They may be quite
different to mine. They may be very simple things. Why not write
them down?

I would like to leave behind:

DON'T LEAVE A MUDDLE

Agnes collected things as some people collect stamps. She died alone, with no close relatives at hand. It fell to her niece, a busy mother, to sort out her affairs. It was a nightmare. Day after day, her niece had to clear and sort things out. She threw away a great deal, but all the time feared that she might get rid of something which some relative might complain about in the future. She became exhausted. Worse, a resentment grew in her which she felt too guilty to acknowledge. It marred her grieving and spoilt her relationship with the one who had died.

Joe and Ivy owned their large, rambling house. Its spare rooms, attic, garage, large garden and shed overflowed with things they had accumulated over their many years together. They declined to move into sheltered housing – they wanted to stay in their familiar home. Then Ivy died, and Joe began to lose his sight. How would he cope with his affairs and his belongings? Would he, like Agnes, bequeath a nightmare to his family or friends?

Joe made a plan. Each week he would sort out a small section of his house or garden. He would think out which friends he could give this or that item to, or he would go to the charity shop or refuse skip. Often I would be cheered when Joe presented me, or the local church, with a plant or object which he had lovingly cleared from his dwelling. It gave us mutual pleasure.

Why not make a plan for the things you have accumulated?

My plan for the things I have accumulated:

MAKE A WILL

Care in planning our resources now and after our death can make all the difference to others. It can create new opportunities for them. It can count for God. Yet over half the people who die have not made a will. They lose the chance to look down from heaven on a work their forethought has made possible.

Even people too poor in life to give away much are worth a lot more at their death, for example through insurance policies or proceeds from the sale of property. Have you thought what good you can continue to do after your death by leaving part of your estate to help further God's work?

If you have relatives who genuinely need your assets (e.g. a dependent spouse), it is a duty to provide for their needs (see 1 Timothy 5:8). In this case, why not leave a residuary bequest of, say, at least a tenth to charity? A residuary bequest is the gift of everything, or a percentage of everything, that is left once all your specified gifts and your debts have been paid.

If your relatives are not in financial need, it is often more appropriate to leave them a memento as a specific bequest, but to give much more to good causes in the form of a residuary bequest. Pray about this, and write into your will what you feel at peace with. You can explain your reasons in the will or in a covering letter.

Here is an example. If you wish to leave a legacy to a charity or church, write out a statement saying:

I leave .... % of my estate to the .... charity, registered no. (if applicable): ....

You may, if you wish, specify that this is to be used for a particular project, charity worker, minister, etc. In that case your solicitor will write a covering letter to the charity to make this clear.

It is possible to purchase a will form from certain stationers and complete it yourself. However, the advice of a solicitor ensures that mistakes and oversights are not made. Most solicitors' charges are reasonable, and they store the will free of charge.

Fill in the checklist of your assets and liabilities at the back of this book (page 235). Save it on a computer disk or make a photocopy, and take it with you to the solicitor. Solicitors tend to charge by the hour, so you save money by having your checklist and your wishes clearly written out in advance.

APPLY THE GOLDEN RULE
TO YOUR DESCENDANTS

This is the Golden Rule: *Do for others what you wish them to do for you.*

What would you wish your descendants to do for you? Would you like them to forget all about you, or would you like them to know about you? To think about you? To mark your life in some way? To pray for you? To show gratitude for something you were, did, wrote or said?

Some non-Western societies have customs which keep them aware of their ancestors. Although it is possible to be tied to ancestors in an unhealthy way, it is also possible to honour them, remember them, and sense a communion with them in a way that does not hinder our own individuality and wholeness.

One way we can do this is to keep our own Book of Remembrance in which we list the anniversaries of relatives' deaths. On each anniversary we can light a candle and remember them. Alternatively, once a year, perhaps around All Souls' Day (2 November), we can light candles in memory of all those in our Book of Remembrance, and take time to recall and savour them.

The advent of the audiovisual age enables us to leave behind 'prints' which will enable our descendants to keep alive their awareness of us. Here are some things we can leave behind:

- A photo album
- A diary
- A video
- Tape recordings
- Letters
- Paintings of, or by, ourselves

EXPRESS YOUR FEELINGS OF LOSS

When we know we shall shortly leave loved ones behind, both we and they suffer grief. Yet often we bottle grief up, which is harmful. Men tend to bottle it up more than women, and British people more than others.

The mass public mourning of the death of Diana, Princess of Wales, broke the mould. Some therapists in the UK reported a 50 per cent drop in referrals in the three months following this. Grieving and crying are good for us. Two weeks after Diana's funeral, I held a workshop on expressing sorrows. A lady in her seventies wrote this prayer:

Dear Lord, please forgive us for locking up our feelings all these years, and help us in future to share our feelings with you.

If we bottle up feelings throughout our lives, it is unlikely that we will be able to express them, as we need to, before we die. If we are wise, we will start now to practise expressing little griefs.

Here is an exercise you can try at any time.

You can probably remember losing a parent, child, pet, close friend or a 'friend' you feel you know through the media. Perhaps you are likely to lose someone in the foreseeable future. Recall or envisage such an experience. Allow to well up feelings of grief at being separated from someone you love. You may find it helpful to play some music that evokes feeling.

What do you feel?

If there are inner tears, let them come out, if they wish to.

What does your heart want to say to the loved one? Speak it out in the safe confines of your private room.

It is important to be real. George Bernard Shaw, writing to Mrs Patrick Campbell on the death of her son, criticized pious words given by a chaplain. In contrast, his words to her were, 'Oh damn, damn, damn, damn, damn, damn, damn, damn, DAMN.'

ACKNOWLEDGE THE
STAGES OF GRIEF

Dr Elisabeth Kübler-Ross's book *On Death and Dying* was a land-mark.[2] Based on her research with dying people, it revealed that four stages of grief are common to many dying people: denial, anger, depression and acceptance. Not every person experiences each stage (those, for example, who grow gently into old age may reach acceptance more easily), but each stage is common to many people.

DENIAL

'It's nothing,' or, 'I'll get better,' or, 'This can't happen to me,' or simply a refusal to talk about it are common reactions. Dr Ross suggests that there is often a need for denial, especially at the beginning of a terminal illness. We should not worry if we go into denial from time to time, but we should worry if we do not move out of it.

ANGER

Anger can be a way to move on from denial. It may be accompanied by envy, self-pity or blame. It gets projected easily onto whoever or whatever is around, causing stress to others. 'Why me?' we ask. In order to assert the fact that we still have a will, we may shout and make demands.

We should not repress or feel guilty about our anger. Being fore-warned, however, we should try to direct it in ways that cause least harm to others. It helps if those around us understand us and give us respect, and help us to talk it through. Yet we need to help ourselves by devising creative strategies, such as the following:

- Vent our anger onto a person who is not physically present, such as Jesus Christ.
- Read or listen to poems or writings that are vehicles for our anger.
- Dictate our angry thoughts onto a Dictaphone.
- Constantly repeat one word that expresses our anger.

DEPRESSION

Some people move out of the second stage by bargaining. They think that if they become 'nice', perhaps they will be spared longer on earth. Others tire of fighting, or lose hope of recovery or of meaning, and sink into depression. Inertia takes over, and with it withdrawal from people.

Yet secretly we may long for a loving hand or voice to reach out to us; for music or conversation or objects of memory to stimulate us. Although visitors should not tire a dying person or stay too long, sensitive interaction often comes as a blessing. Depression can be eased when we dwell on things in our past we feel good about, or when we get off our chests things we need to offload.

ACCEPTANCE

If we have been able to express our feelings at each of these stages, and to mourn our impending loss of the things on earth we hold most dear, the gift of peace may be ours.

This is not mere resignation ('I can't keep this up') – it is co-operation ('I am ready to go'). This acceptance may be devoid of feelings which in life we describe as 'happy', but it is free of fear or despair.

At this stage we may no longer want surface distractions such as television, and we only want short visits. Touch and a brief word mean more than chatter. The journey into separation from this life is underway.

These cycles of emotion should not be strangers to us when we die. If we rehearse them while we are in health, they can be 'old friends' when we are dying.

BE REAL

When life gets unpleasant, we seek escape in fantasy. When we avoid reality, we easily build castles in the air. It is only too easy to surround death with treacly sentiment, and to imagine that heaven will be whatever we want it to be. If we do this, we miss the pain which is the precondition for growth. We miss the depths and the meaning of life. In fact, we miss the boat!

The writer C.S. Lewis had a brief, deeply loving marriage. He was able to share so many aspects of his life with his wife Joy, but then she died an untimely death from cancer. This was featured in the film *Shadowlands*.

In his little book *A Grief Observed*, Lewis recounts how neither he nor she would allow unreal sentiment or nostalgia to blanket the harsh reality of parting. He concluded that they could never have a rerun of their times together on earth: 'all that talk of family reunions' in heaven was nonsense. He believed that heaven was that state 'when the former things have passed away', so they had to accept the finality of their physical parting.[3]

Being real is a necessary part of our preparation for death and life.

FREE THE TRAPPED SPIRIT

Sometimes life can feel like a cage. We feel trapped. We must find a way of getting free before we die. There is nothing worse than to die with our spirit still trapped. People whose spirits are trapped at death can come back to haunt us.

The priest's phone rang. 'It's the police. A situation has developed in the new street in your parish which we can't handle. Can you help?' A husband had committed suicide in the garage of a single mother living opposite. The following day one after another of the new street's residents became hysterical: they each swore they had seen the dead man. The new life of a streetful of residents was in jeopardy.

The local priest did two things. First, he took a cross into each disturbed home and asked Jesus to take the spirit of the deceased into his care, and to take the people of the house under his protection. Second, he held a private service of Holy Communion for the deceased (a requiem), so that his trapped or restless spirit would be freed.

There was no further disturbance.

Dr Kenneth McAll has done some research on unquiet spirits. He concluded that the unexplained disturbances in the infamous Bermuda Triangle might have been caused by unquiet spirits. Innumerable slaves who died while being shipped across the sea in that area were dumped overboard without any Christian funeral. He held a mass Christian funeral and Communion service for them on a ship, and claimed that from then until the time of his writing there were no fatalities in the Bermuda Triangle.

How can we make sure that when we depart this earth we are free in spirit?

We can say from our hearts, while we are in health, some words from Christian worship which release a soul to God:

> You, Christ, are the King of glory.
> You are the everlasting Son of the Father.
> When you overcame the sting of death
> You opened the gate of heaven to all believers.

Come then, Lord, to the aid of your people.
We are bought with the price of your own precious blood.
Bring us with your saints to glory everlasting.[4]

RELEASE COMPASSION

Our spirits become trapped when our emotions become blocked. This may be because we hold something against other people, or because we repress deep, unfulfilled aspirations.

If this is true of us when we realize we have not long to live, we may assume that there is now nothing we can do about this. So we become more hard, more repressed or suicidal. We may sink into such depression that we refuse to communicate with others.

There is something we can do, however. It is never too late to release the compassion which is locked up inside us. People who spontaneously express compassion have no idea what good they do.

The final act of a man dying of AIDS was to kiss the hand of a carer. His last words were, 'Friendship is what matters most to me.'

Do not die with the ocean of compassion that belongs to you still locked inside you. Practise expressing your compassion day by day. The simplest, most basic words, such as 'Sorry', 'I love you', 'Thank you', or 'Tell her I'll never forget her', wing their way to the other person's heart and carry healing in their wings.

Speak from your heart to someone today.

LISTEN TO YOUR DREAMS

Some dreams, especially those that recur or that remain vivid in waking life, tell us about our fears, futures or choices.

A client revealed to psychologist Carl Jung a dream of climbing a mountain and then mounting upwards into the empty air. The man, a mountaineer, awoke in ecstasy after the dream. Jung advised him not to go climbing alone. He ignored the advice, and was buried in an avalanche, then rescued. Not long afterwards, when he was out climbing again, he was killed while descending a rock face.

Jung was not surprised by such dreams, for he believed that anything that will be happens on the basis of what has been. Nonetheless, the fact that he advised clients to take precautions indicates that we need not be fatalistic: we can steer our predispositions.

An unmarried man in outwardly good health and not yet retired became depressed. He felt within himself that, like his parents before him, he would become ill and die before he was old. Yet he rebelled against the thought of dying. 'Why should I react in this way against dying when it can be a natural fulfilment?' he asked himself.

A woman's near-death experience gave him a clue. A spirit being told her that we subconsciously choose what happens in our bodies, including when we die. That man realized that he was wedded to his work and that, if that ceased, he would have nothing to live for, since his work compensated for the repressed areas of his life. He could choose death (to go on as he was) or life (to engage with those repressed aspects of his life).

That night he had a dream. A successful person, dressed in bright, eighteenth-century costume, was sitting in a carriage that went forward at a good walking pace. The dreamer himself was a bystander. Unexpectedly, a very small carriage caught up and came alongside the main carriage. It turned out to be the cortege of an infant.

The man awoke, and tried to interpret his dream. The small cortege, he felt, signified the life that he had never lived. Taken literally, it might mean that it was too late, it was now dead for ever. If that was so, however, why did it unexpectedly come into view? The dream was telling him that there was, indeed, a life that he had not lived. Yet the fact that it had come into view encouraged him to pray that it *would* come to life, as the prophet Elisha prayed over the corpse of a boy and brought him back to life.

From that time on, the man daily looked for little ways to engage with his repressed life. The fatalism with which he had assumed an early death disappeared. He also began to look upon his eventual death as a fulfilment rather than as a threat.

AT THE FIRST GLIMPSE
OF DEATH'S APPROACH

When I first glimpse the approach of death, what do I do? Many people respond in one of these ways:

- 'I'm frightened. Help me.'
- 'It's not fair.'
- 'Give me time to be angry.'
- 'I don't want to be alone.'
- 'Come to me, friends on earth. Come to me, friends in heaven.'
- 'I believe. Help my unbelief.'
- 'Lord, have mercy on me.'

Each of us is unique, however, and we may respond in a way that is unique to ourselves.

Write down here what you think you will want to say:

Now think about these words of St Paul:

> More than anything else, we wish to please the Lord, whether in
> our home here or there. For all of us must appear before Christ,
> to be judged by him. Each one will receive what he deserves.
> 2 CORINTHIANS 5:9,10

THE HEALING POWER
OF ACCEPTANCE

Many people die quickly or quietly in their sleep. Others linger, unable to look after themselves. Sometimes, on a sleepless night, we may wonder which it will be for us.

My aged friend Frank Rowland was most capable and in full control throughout his long life, and seldom suffered fools gladly. He outlived his wife, and many of his friends, until his world was reduced to a bed in a nursing home. Lying on his bed, he scribbled this poem:

> I've sometimes wondered as I lie
> Why I am not allowed to die:
> Why others who are yet more ill
> Are given strength to linger still.
> I know the reason why we're kept:
> It is to teach us to accept.

There is healing power in acceptance. A boy who was dying of leukaemia spoke with calm inner authority to some adults. 'What I need,' he said, 'is for people to treat me as if I were not ill – for them to laugh and have fun with me and just be natural.'

PREPARE TO LEAVE

There are four ingredients in a goodbye that is true.

First, we need to accept that we have to go. We need to take time to feel our pain and loss, and to acknowledge it.

Second, we need to look inward. If we are used to living on the outside, this is a new experience. Tell yourself that it is OK, in fact it is the right and good thing, to slow down, to have times of solitude and stillness. When you do this, you become aware of your conflicting feelings. In the spaces you create for yourself, express these feelings, silently or aloud.

Third, we need to act out our leave-taking. Symbols and actions can sometimes express what words cannot. For example, we could go for a walk or for an imaginary journey, and deposit stones or items that symbolize what we have to leave. We could touch trees or flowers on the journey to symbolize people we need to touch and speak to before we move on.

Fourth, we need to connect with the deep wellspring inside ourselves which nourishes us for the coming journey that we have never made before. Jesus went up a mountain and communed with beings of light (Moses and Elijah) before his death. This transfigured the way he faced death. His face shone with joy, despite the fact that he was to suffer a torturous end. By quietly and calmly opening ourselves to this inner wellspring, this divine light, we receive it into our conscious being.

PLAN THE FUNERAL

A funeral, although sad, should be a fitting farewell and, if you are a believer, a faith-building experience for your friends and family.

Too often numbed relatives, a commercialized funeral industry and a minister who may be ignorant of personal details result in a strange, impersonal service that leaves mourners empty and does not do justice to the unique character of the deceased. Sometimes relatives fall out before the funeral because the deceased has not made clear what type of disposal or funeral he or she would prefer.

You can avoid all this by making your wishes clear. These days many funeral firms have schemes you can buy into, such as a funeral bond. You choose your type and price of coffin, hearse, etc. and begin to make regular payments.

A growing number of people exercise their right to arrange funerals without using a funeral director. I know one man who ordered his cardboard coffin from a catalogue, and kept it under the sofa. He and his wife arranged their own funeral cars and chose a burial site through a local church.

Keeping a coffin in the house is not to everyone's taste, of course, but it does have the added advantage of keeping us familiar with death. I have a prayer corner in which I keep my deed box and funeral instructions, which serves a similar purpose.

A friend of mine recently sent me details of a mother-in-law who had just died. On the card were listed the names of each of her children and grandchildren, and their addresses. I was invited to say 'farewell' at her flat on the afternoon before the funeral.

It is good to plan some of your funeral yourself. Some people even write their own service. It is also helpful, however, to allow your loved ones some scope in planning it. The service is for their benefit too.

Have you thought about where you wish your funeral to be? In a local church, perhaps, or are you interested in the new movement for woodland funerals?[1] Fill out the funeral arrangements form at the back of this book (see page 236), and scan it onto your computer or make photocopies. Give these to your next of kin and, if you know a minister or funeral director well, to them also. Alternatively – because you may change your mind later about some details – keep the form up to date in an accessible place, and tell these people that you have filled out such a form.

CELEBRATE A LIFE

A human life is too wonderful to be bid farewell in one short funeral service. Why not hold a service first which provides plenty of room and time, then follow that with a short, private ceremony at the crematorium or graveyard for a few close family members and friends?

Or have you considered holding a memorial event after the funeral? This gives you time to prepare. Famous people do it, and you are a VIP too, in your own way. People who have known the deceased at different times of life can write or record memories, or pay tributes through words, songs or the gift of something personal. Children can make drawings and present these. A photographic, audio or video record can be compiled.

In Indiana, Indians appoint a Speaker for the deceased. He or she listens to the memories of the mourners and records them. Then, at a wake, the Speaker recounts these memories for some 90 minutes. Traditionally, the Irish hold a more informal time of eating, drinking and reminiscing. Why not jot down your own ideas for a wake or celebration of your life?

WHEN WOULD YOU LIKE
TO BE REMEMBERED?

Here is an idea from Orthodox Christianity. As well as the yearly anniversary of a departed soul, they also keep a special remembrance on the third, ninth and fortieth days after death. These days link up with realities which join heaven to earth – so it may be that after your death you are aware of these special remembrances.

THE THIRD DAY

Christ rose from death on the third day, so the emphasis of this day should be songs, prayers and readings of praise and resurrection. Think also that the reposed person received his or her being through the Trinity, and through the resurrection will be able to reflect more fully the Three-fold Love.

> O Trinity of love and power,
> Immortal Life of every soul,
> Your dearest child now comes to flower
> And reaches their eternal goal.

THE NINTH DAY

On the ninth day after death, remember both the reposed and his or her friends who remain. The ninth day is chosen because in the next world there are nine orders of spirit beings, or angels, who offer three-times-three devotions to God and, being drawn to God, embrace those whom God is drawing to himself. On this day, think how the reposed is being united with the company of heaven.

Imagine someone you love offering you up thus:

> With the angels and saints, my dear one,
> You cry holy, holy, holy
> to the Lord who was, and is, and is to come.
> You are caught up in heaven's harmony of praise.
> You are sharing in its glory.

THE FORTIETH DAY

Memorial is made on the fortieth day because God's people did this with faithful friends such as Moses, and because the risen Christ finally left the earth on the fortieth day after his resurrection.

* * *

Would you like to be remembered at any particular time or in any particular way? If so, you might like to note this below.

How I would like to be remembered:

'HONOUR ME,
DON'T HUMOUR ME'

The worst kind of prison is not being able to share 'terminal feelings' with those we love. Many well-meaning relatives won't talk about death in front of a dying person. They may think they are protecting that person, but all too often they are protecting themselves.

Some doctors, because they have been trained to cure and feel that not to cure is to fail, refuse to tell patients the truth about their condition. Most, though not all of us do know deep down when we are dying, and we want to be able to talk about it.

Suppose we are dying, and we are surrounded by people who are falsely 'protecting' us? It is hard when we are weak, confused or sedated to take the initiative, so it can be helpful to work out now the sort of thing we would want to say then.

To my dearest I would want to say something like this:

Dearest,
    I want you to honour me, not to humour me. You honour me by believing that I want to face reality.

To my doctor I would want to say this:

Dear Doctor
    If you want to help me, don't be distant, don't be in denial. You are a human being first and a doctor second. Trust me with the truth. Spare me the gory details, but give me the nub. When you make your daily round, I don't want a view of your legs; I want to see your face. I want you to be a gracious, not a grating presence. You are a mortal, like me. Our shared mortality binds us together.

If you wish, write down here what you will want to say to your dearest and to your doctor, and what you would like them to say to you.

HOW TO SAY WHAT
WE WANT TO SAY

Many of us, before we die, wish to say things to our nearest and dearest, or maybe even to those who have become distant as a result of some hurt. The trouble is, our mouths won't speak what our hearts want to say. Why?

Perhaps we fear it will release emotions in ourselves that we won't know how to manage. Perhaps we fear to upset the one who will be left behind. Perhaps there are skeletons in the cupboard. By pretending everything will be all right, and by not speaking about death or the deeper things, we keep a veneer of calm, but at the price of an unsatisfactory parting.

A key to solving this problem is for each person to work out, either on their own or with a friend, *what* it is they want to say. For the moment, it does not matter *how, when,* or even *if* you say it – just get clear what you want to say. Then write it down or tell it to a friend.

Once you are clear what you want to say, some of the fears and confusions will fall away. The next step is to plan how to say it. Some people write it down. If what you want to say is really difficult, a third person could read what you have written to the person concerned, but if possible it is best to say it person to person.

Sometimes, of course, the person you want to talk to may be far away. Why not speak your thoughts into a tape recorder?

A husband was dying. Neither he nor his wife could talk about it. Something had to give, and the wife took it out on the hospital staff. 'She's a bad therapist. She made him stop walking,' complained the wife.

A nurse with empathy asked her, 'Is it because you want your husband to get better that you're scared, if the therapist doesn't push him, he won't get stronger?'

Wife (crying): 'Yes, I'm scared!'

Nurse: 'Are you scared of losing him?'

Wife: 'Yes, we've been together for so long.'

Nurse: 'Are you worrying about how you would feel if he dies?'

Wife: 'I just can't imagine how long I'm going to live without him. He's always been there for me. Always.'

Having faced what was really troubling her, the wife was better able to come to terms with her husband dying, and to talk with him directly. This made it easier for him – and for the therapist.

DEAR GRACE, WHEN I AM DYING...

This is the sort of letter I would write to a friend if I found out today that I was shortly to die:

Dear Grace,

When I am dying, will you, if you are able, come and be beside me?

In my frailty my weakest traits may come out. Frustrations, depression, anger, regrets, may rise to the surface. May I pour them out to you knowing that you will not reject me?

If these negative emotions get misdirected onto you, please understand that I know the real you has only love for me.

Remind me that I am a loved child of God, that I was born in love and shall end in love, with you, a being of love alongside me.

Will you hold my hand or head, and stroke me if I ask you to?

You are a friend indeed.

Ray

SAYING OUR GOODBYES

In an ideal world, the struggle to live is followed by acceptance that death is near, a letting go of this life, and the saying of farewells.

Those who are dying need the permission of the living to die. When such permission is given, it makes it easier for the dying person to let go and the dying becomes more peaceful. Some relatives can do this, but some just can't. If your intuition tells you that your relatives do not give you permission, why not ask a third party, such as a home carer or a chaplain, to tell your family that you know you are dying, you want them to know that you are ready, and it's OK for them to let go?

If religious language is not for you, you can use informal words such as, 'It's OK for me to go,' or, 'You can let me go now; I'll always love you.'

Goodbyes can be spaced out, too, leaving until last the persons who will be with you to the end.

PARTING GIFTS

Little things given with thought can mean much more than expensive items given without thought. Before he died, my uncle gave me a packet of unused underpants!

Perhaps a friend or relative has made a comment about something of yours, such as 'I love that', and this can prompt you to bequeath it to them for its sentimental value.

If you are not sure what to give someone, you could ask directly, 'Is there anything you would like?'

Of course, a parting gift need not be an object. It can be a kiss, a conversation, a prayer, a phone call – anything.

EPITAPHS

Once I was as you are now...
You will be as I am now.

This is part of a famous epitaph on a tombstone. It was written by the deceased in order to prompt passers-by to live their lives in the light of eternity.

Generally, epitaphs are written by the next of kin, not by the person who has died, but there are exceptions. This light-hearted piece written by Benjamin Franklin is one such:

The body of
Benjamin Franklin, printer,
(Like the cover of an old book,
Its contents worn out,
And stripped of its lettering and gilding)
Lies here, food for worms!
Yet the work itself shall not be lost,
For it will, as he believed, appear once more,
In a new
And more beautiful edition,
Corrected and amended
By its Author!

In my opinion, it is best to let your next of kin provide an epitaph for your own gravestone or crematorium plaque, or to write something in a Book of Remembrance, unless you have a very strong conviction to suggest something for them to consider.

If you have to provide an epitaph for a deceased loved one, how do you decide what is appropriate? What if the deceased was a difficult person?

Why not pick out one quality which is distinctive of the deceased, and worth remembering? When my Dad died, we found a poem he had handwritten on a piece of paper. It included these words, which we chose to put on his tombstone in Aldingbourne churchyard, West Sussex:

Fearless since my Saviour lives.

Although it is not generally a good idea to take control of your own public epitaph, it *is* a good idea to write an imaginary epitaph for your own private use. I find this helps me to focus on what is the most important thing in my life.

What would you like people to say about you after you are gone? I like this epitaph:

He did all things well.

This was said about Jesus, and could not in truth be said about me, even though I aim for it. I like this epitaph also, which – you never know – might just become true:

Nothing became him like his departing.

This was said about King Charles II, who was thought by many to have fudged the right courses of action in his life, but who died most nobly.

Questions that can help us write a private epitaph for ourselves include:

- What was I put on this earth for?
- What mark would I like to leave on it?
- What longing, quality or calling is deepest in me?
- What talent or concern has most moved me?
- How would I like people to remember me?

Write a private epitaph for yourself below:

This exercise may bring to light things that need to be resolved. It may point you to what you need to work at most in your life in order to achieve your destiny.

A WAY TO MEDITATE AT DEATH

Bring to mind the spiritual figure of light and love who means most to you, and invite that figure to be present to you. I choose to invoke the figure of Christ. If you cannot envisage a figure clearly, focus on a Presence of light and love.

Picture the negative thoughts, experiences and blockages being taken away, dissolved and transformed by the Presence of light. The light is so filling you that you are becoming a being of light.

The rays of light are now rays of forgiveness and inner healing. Picture yourself being forgiven and made whole. Let every memory of your life that wants to do so parade itself before the Presence of light.

You can now depart this life without ties of hostility holding you back. Bless all the people who flash through your mind, and bring them into the Presence of light.

Open yourself to the heart of this Presence of light. Allow yourself to be drawn nearer to it. Your earth friends and earth ties are becoming more distant. You are leaving them behind and you are going towards eternal love.

FUN ON THE WAY OUT

Don't misunderstand me: I know that dying can be far from pleasant. Yet, however difficult it may be, it can always be seasoned with humour or hope.

My aged friend Margaret Fish said, 'I do not fear death, but my body is like an old banger, and I did fear going out in this old banger. Then the Lord told me, "Don't worry, I'm in the banger with you, and when it's time to get out, I'll get out with you!"'

My young friend Nigel, whose story is told later, learned that he would shortly die of inoperable cancer. He went down to the depths, but he also climbed to the heights. In hospital he joked with the staff to cheer them up, and talked to friends about his 'heavenly career'.

A dying man told his friend that he was worried about what lay on the other side of death. Just then his dog scratched at the door, wanting to come in. 'Your dog doesn't know what lies on the other side of this door,' his friend told him, 'except that his master is there. That's all he needs to know. Your master is on the other side of death's door. That is enough.'

The Irish like to remind people, 'We will have good weather after the final raindrop.'

LAST WISHES

Please take the trouble to think out what your wishes are for each relative or friend whom you carry in your heart. Then find a way to communicate this, through words spoken or written down.

This is what a Czech resistance worker wanted to say to his infant son Jan. He wrote it in a letter to his wife before he was executed in March 1944:

> Teach our son courage. Let him have an immediate approach to everything about him. Teach him to enjoy victory over hatred and envy. It needs courage to have a pure heart. He should excel in the art of tolerance – thus will he find faith in himself and God.[6]

The Antarctic explorer Captain Robert Scott, knowing that he was dying of frostbite and cold, wrote this to his great friend J.M. Barrie:

> Goodbye, I am not at all afraid of the end, but sad to miss many a humble pleasure which I had planned for the future ... I never met a man in my life whom I admired and loved more than you, and I could never show you how much your friendship meant to me, for you had much to give and I nothing.[7]

FINAL WORDS

We cannot be certain that we shall be in a position to say what we want to say to friends and family at the end of our lives, but it is best to be prepared.

Christopher Probst wrote this to his mother and sister:

> I thank you for having given me life. When I really think it through it has been a single road to God. Do not grieve that I must now skip the last part of it. Soon I shall be closer to you than before. In the meantime I'll prepare a glorious reception for you all.[8]

Many a person has breathed words such as these at their last:

- 'Thank you.'
- 'I'm sorry.'
- 'Forgive me.'
- 'Be true.'
- 'I love you.'

The following famous piece puts into words what some people want to say. One person left a copy of this on a card with this scribbled note: 'This card says all I want to say.'

> Death is nothing at all … I have only slipped away into the next room. I am I and you are you – whatever we were to each other, that we are still. Call me by my old familiar name, speak to me in the easy way you always used. Put no difference into your tone; wear no forced air of solemnity or sorrow. Laugh as we always laughed at the little jokes we enjoyed together. Play, smile, think of me, pray for me … Why should I be out of mind because I am out of sight? I am but waiting for you, for an interval, somewhere very near, just around the corner. All is well. Nothing is past; nothing is lost. One brief moment and all will be as before.
>
> HENRY SCOTT HOLLAND

Some people die feeling content and their last words express this contentment. 'This is the last of earth. I am content,' said John Quincy Adams. Douglas Fairbanks simply said, 'I've never felt better!'

People who have no clear faith in God may choose to look back, rather than forward, so that both they and the one they leave behind remember some moment of past happiness. I do not know what Linda McCartney's last words to her husband Paul were, but we do know his last words to her. He tried to conjure up for her a picture of the free spirit she was when she was with her horses in the Appalachian mountains: 'You were up on your beautiful Appaloosa stallion. It's a fine spring day, we're riding through the woods. The bluebells are all out and the sky is clear blue.' Sir Paul insisted that Linda's two ponies were led to the front of St Martin-in-the-Fields Church, London, at her memorial service.[9]

Those who do have a strong faith may want to mention the future as well as the past. The scientist Thomas Edison's last words were, 'It is very beautiful over there.'

Now try to think about what you would like to say to each of your loved ones before you die. Write it down here:

FAREWELL BLESSINGS

What could be nicer than to know that, before someone you love passed on, they thought about you and wanted to bless you?

To bless means that you want the best for a person as they really are. It does no good giving someone a product or a word that does not connect with their true wellbeing. To bless friends or family requires us to think about them: their character, their possibilities, their talents, their way of relating to others, their temperament, their style.

The Bible gives us inside information about blessings on a grand scale given by the Grand Old Man Jacob to each of his children and grandchildren. He foretold that his son Judah's offspring would be like a lion whom nations would honour. Zebulun's family would become seaside dwellers, but Issachar's family would end up in slavery (see Genesis 49).

Most of us will give blessings or discernments on a smaller scale, but we can give them with as much care and thought as Jacob did.

AN EXERCISE

Visualize someone you love – as they were, as they are now, and as they could be in 10 years' time if the best in them blossoms. Take a few minutes to do this.

Can you put this into words, or into a picture (either in your mind or on paper)?

Is there something you could give them that will show them what you mean?

Is there some object that comes to mind when you think of them?

Pick out a quality you think is good. It could be strong, or weak but capable of growing strong. Say the following: 'I bless you (or God bless you) with the quality of ....'

You can practise giving thoughtful gifts or blessings each year, at Christmas or birthdays.

Why not prepare thoughtful words or gifts for loved ones now? Try filling in the list below.

If I were to die now, I would want to give these things or blessings to these loved ones:

Person

Thing

Words

ANOINTED FOR BURIAL

Preparing to die well is not the same thing as making the best of a bad job. It is possible for our death to be anointed and to be a blessing to others.

Royal people, holy people and people embarking on a great mission are anointed with oil – oil that brings fragrance and affirms a calling. We too may be anointed, outwardly or inwardly, for that great commission we call death.

Even people who suffer untimely and gruesome deaths can be inwardly anointed by God. A small community of new Christians in Cambodia poured their lives out so that the people of Cambodia might find God, and they met daily to soak themselves in the Scriptures, prayer and God. They were brutally killed by the Khmer Rouge, along with millions of others, in the 'Killing Fields' of Cambodia. Their deaths seemed senseless, yet with hindsight they seemed to mark a turning point. Before the slaughter of that community, Cambodia had only a small number of rather defensive Christians. Following it, hundreds of thousands became caring, outgoing Christians.

The book which tells their story is entitled *Anointed for Burial*. Those who continued their work believe that God used those people's deaths to draw many others into the life of God, and that they were inwardly anointed for death. This reminds me of the saying, 'The blood of the martyrs is the seedbed of the Church.'

Those Cambodian Christians were not outwardly anointed. A young Palestinian who died an untimely and gruesome death was so anointed, however. His name was Jesus. The famous Nativity story of the 'three kings' tells how one of them, even though Jesus was only an infant, brought a gift of myrrh, which was used for anointing at death (see Matthew 2:11). Thirty years later, a woman friend poured costly anointing oil over Jesus. Vast crowds had acclaimed him that day, but she sensed that the day was a prelude to his death. She anointed him for his burial.

Jesus' death indeed proved to be 'anointed', more than any death before or since. Out of it came resurrection, not just for himself, but, in a different sense, also for his followers and for the world. From the Tree of Death grew the Tree of Life.

There is a principle here which Jesus taught and which can apply to us. Jesus said, 'Unless a seed is buried in the ground and dies, it remains just a single seed; but if it dies, it bears much fruit' (John 12:24). Knowing about this amazing principle can create a desire in us to be anointed for our burial in a way which – although unknown to us and not controlled by us – will somehow lead to life for others after our death.

God alone is responsible for any good that may come out of our death, but we have the privilege of receiving anointing for our burial. How do we receive this? We receive it both inwardly and outwardly.

INWARD ANOINTING

For inward anointing, we immerse ourselves in Scripture and meditations; we invite God's Holy Spirit to fill us, at conscious and unconscious levels, so that our lives become an outpouring.

Jesus as Son of God is eternally pouring out his life in sacrificial love. We are called to be joined to him in this pouring out of our lives. Jesus was anointed to do this on earth through the living out of a deep, intimate relationship with his Father God, which meant death to selfish things, but life in every other way. This is a deep mystery. If we are given understanding, however, we can prepare ourselves for death by making ourselves one with Jesus.

It may help us to repeat often, from our heart, the psalm which Jesus spoke from his memory and from his heart as he died:

My God, my God, why have you forsaken me?...
O my God, I cry by day, but you do not answer;
and by night, but find no rest.
Yet you are holy,
enthroned on the praises of Israel...
It was you who took me from the womb;
you kept me safe on my mother's breast.
On you I was cast from my birth,
and since my mother bore me you have been my God.
Do not be far from me,
for trouble is near
and there is no one to help...
I am poured out like water,

and all my bones are out of joint;
my heart is like wax;
it is melted within my breast;
my mouth is dried up like a potsherd,
and my tongue sticks to my jaws;
you lay me in the dust of death...
But you, O LORD, do not be far away!
O my help, come quickly to my aid!
Deliver my soul from the sword,
my life from the power of the dog!
Save me from the mouth of the lion!...
All the ends of the earth shall remember and turn to the LORD...
To him, indeed, shall all who sleep in the earth bow down...
and I shall live for him.
Posterity will serve him;
future generations will be told about the LORD,
and proclaim his deliverance to a people yet unborn,
saying that he has done it.

VERSES FROM PSALM 22, NRSV

Christians can also be inwardly anointed for death by renewing their baptism, which means drowning the ego and immersing themselves in God's Presence. A way to do this is to picture ourselves wading into water, leaving behind the past, immersing ourselves in God, and praying: 'Lord, I invite your Holy Spirit to fill me and overflow me with that life which is eternal, to inflame me with that fire which can never be extinguished.'

We can also use this prayer of dedication:

I dedicate my death.
I will offer it as an act of love to all.
I dedicate any pain my death may entail.
May my pain be a bridge between the pain of innumerable people
    and God.
I breathe in the suffering of others.
I breathe out the Spirit of Christ.

Practise breathing the Spirit onto others as Christ did (see John 20:22).

Do not be shy of asking a priest, pastor or soul friend to anoint you with oil for your death. Seek to know within yourself the right time to do this. Some may feel the inspiration to receive an anointing while in health; others may ask for it when they realize that they are dying.

The forehead and the palms of the hands may be signed in oil with the cross. Hands may be laid on the head. The following words may be said slowly during the anointing and repeated.

Death with oil
Death with joy
Death with light
Death with penitence
Death with gladness
Death without pain
Death without fear
Death without death
Death without horror
Death without grieving.

CARMINA GADELICA[10]

If you receive such an anointing, you may wish to spend time afterwards praising God, and enjoying the Presence of the holy and eternal Carer.

CHOOSE YOUR TIME TO GO

A doctor or friend informs a patient, 'There is no more medical treatment available.'

'Then I must die?' says the patient.

'We all have to die. Your time left is getting shorter.'

'But I want to live.'

'Then do live. Live fully every day you are given.'

'If I have to die soon, I shall aim to live until I have seen and said and done certain things.'

'Yes, that is good.'

On 1 January 2001 people lined the eastern edge of Lindisfarne, waiting for the sun to rise. Among them was a lady who was dying of cancer. 'I wanted to live long enough to see the sun rise on Holy Island at the start of a new millennium,' she explained. The sun leaped across the shimmering sea and bathed her and all of us in welcoming glory. Now she could die.

The nun Thérèse of Lisieux had a passion to be a priest, but females were not permitted to be priests at that time. She channelled her passion in both a conscious and an unconscious way. The conscious way was to pray for the souls of priests she knew. The unconscious way was to die on the exact date she would have been ordained a priest if she had been a man. That is rather dramatic, but all sorts of dying people aim to live until a birth, marriage, anniversary, meeting, reconciliation or goodbye takes place.

Those who are in touch with themselves or with God often sense when God will take them. We become more sensitive to inner 'changes of gear'. If we develop such a sensitivity, we are more likely to know the right moment to leave this world.

When Jacob ended his charge to his sons, he drew up his feet into the bed, breathed his last, and was gathered to his people (see Genesis 49:33).

A fear expressed by some people is that the time of death of a person in the terminal stages of an illness might be planned for the convenience of hospital staff. For example, pain-killing drugs which induce death might be given to fit in with reduced staffing periods such as Christmas or a weekend. If, however, death is a mysterious process towards a transcendent state, profound events may be taking place at the unconscious and semi-conscious level in a patient, and these should be allowed to take their course.

If you feel strongly about this, write a note about it below and ask someone close to you to make a copy and give it to the medical staff if ever this situation arises.

Dear Hospital Staff,

Signed:

Date:

EARLY EXIT OR ENCORE?

Some of the best television or theatre shows gradually build up to their climax. Perhaps a presenter says, 'We're coming to the end,' and this is the cue for each person to make their final contribution. In the theatre there may be a grand finale, followed by cheers and cries of 'Encore!' Highlights from the entire show are then repeated before the curtain finally falls, to the satisfaction of all.

We should be prepared for the possibility that we will be given the chance of an 'encore' before we die. Some of us slip away earlier than expected, and that is that. Others rally unexpectedly and experience intense energy and awareness before the end. This is an opportunity to recap great moments of our life, to recall, say or do things we overlooked first time round, and to repeat farewells, perhaps in the presence of more people, or simply being more present to a few.

A famous violinist was asked why he practised several hours a day at the age of 95. 'Because I am still improving,' he replied. If God permits, we can go on improving and know the joy of an encore.

ON THE DAY DEATH
KNOCKS AT THE DOOR

On the day when death knocks at my door, what shall I offer the Keeper of death either in the closing minutes of this life or in the opening minutes of my new birth in the life beyond?

I will set before God:

all the lovely things that I have seen,

all the love that I have received and given,

all the insights of truth that I have gathered,

all the things that I have valued and enjoyed,

all the tasks completed or left for others,

all my gratitude and love for the past,

all my content in the present,

and my hope for the future.

Above all, I will offer my recognition of the Lord who has come in the guise of death, to lead me to the home God has prepared for me."

In order to do these things on my last day, I need to practise doing them now.

Why not take time to rehearse in your mind, or to write down, the things suggested above?

On the day death knocks at my door I will set before God:

PART FOUR

* * *

CREATE A GOOD 'DEPARTURE LOUNGE'

DRAW UP YOUR 'DEPARTURE LOUNGE' GUIDELINES

In a large airport an announcer asks passengers, when the time of their flight departure approaches, to leave the main concourse and make their way to the departure lounge. This is smaller and quieter than the main concourse. Passengers are usually not detained there long, although occasionally the flight is delayed. Then the departure lounge comes into deeper focus.

A wise person prepares a suitable 'departure lounge' for their final flight from earth. This part of the book explores the 'rooms' we may need in our 'departure lounge'.

It is important to create a good atmosphere around us as we prepare to leave this life. If heaven is the ultimate in love, beauty, peace, truth and creativity, then we should surround ourselves with those things as we approach its threshold.

Sogyal Rinpoche observes in his book *The Tibetan Book of Living and Dying* that it was normal for Tibetans to create a harmonious environment around the dying, but this is often lacking in the West. To create an atmosphere of calm, warmth, beauty and openness around a dying person is one of the most beautiful things we can do.

Wherever possible, a person should die in a home or hospice, where loved ones can stay overnight. In some hospitals there is no privacy, and there is little chance of the body being undisturbed for a period after death. In intensive care units, dying patients may be hooked up to monitors, and attempts to resuscitate them will be made when they stop breathing which interrupt the natural rhythm of dying. Nevertheless, even in a hospital, with imagination and clear requests to the staff, a helpful atmosphere can be created.

When our turn to depart comes, we need to have some guidelines ready, since our loved ones may not know what we would like or who is responsible for shaping the environment around us.

I have produced some simple guidelines on my computer which I can print out and give to anyone who can help to create my 'departure lounge'. If by chance I have a sudden stroke and cannot speak, I ask my nearest to look in the file marked 'Personal'. At the moment these are mere jottings. As I think more about this, no doubt I will make these clearer and fuller.

RAY SIMPSON'S 'DEPARTURE LOUNGE' GUIDELINES FOR LOVED ONES AND CARERS

- Yes, flowers, grapes and a favourite drink are nice, but also something fragrant, please, such as the scent of lilac, honeysuckle or lavender.
- I wish to look at something that has had meaning to me over a long time, such as a favourite painting, family or neighbourhood photograph, or ikon of Christ.
- I would like to listen to taped messages from friends which I could listen to if and when I felt up to it, and to favourite pieces of music.
- I would like persons with whom I feel a rapport to be with me, to hold my hand or to stroke me, to talk, but also to cease to talk, and to know when to just sit or pray or depart.
- If I have to be in an intensive care unit, once it is known that there is no chance of recovery, have me moved to a private room and discontinue injections and invasive procedures before the very end. It is vital the mind is calm immediately before death.
- After my death, leave the body undisturbed for as long as possible.
- Peaceful death is a human right.

Once you have read through the rest of this chapter, write down what you would like in your own 'departure lounge'.

....................'S 'DEPARTURE LOUNGE' GUIDELINES FOR LOVED ONES AND CARERS

The kind of atmosphere I would like on my deathbed is:

Some things I would like around me are:

ANYTHING TO DECLARE?

The rest of this section explores possibilities for some of the 'rooms', but before we can enter the departure lounge we have to be searched and to say if we have anything to declare.

Everyone has to be searched, but some people travel light and don't have to worry about declarations. Others need to do so. If you need to get things off your chest, there are various ways of doing this. Some do it within themselves, or face to face with a person they have wronged, or with God. Some retire into a corner and listen to a recording of a penitential litany being said or sung.

Others ask for a priest, pastor or soul friend to whom they can confess. If you choose to do this, the following form of words may be used.

CONFESSIONS

The dying person is here described as 'Pilgrim' and the person in whom they confide is described as 'Minister'. The Pilgrim may name persons or sins, or, if they cannot speak, squeeze the minister's hands to signify 'yes'.

Minister: Do you wish to be forgiven for failings throughout your life, even those you are not conscious of?
Pilgrim: Yes.
Minister: Christ have mercy.
Pilgrim: Christ have mercy.
Minister: God of compassion, in your goodness pardon all sins now forgotten, and blot these out from your record.

Minister: Is there any person now living to whom you wish to be reconciled?
Pilgrim: Yes.
Minister: Do you forgive this person and in your heart ask them to forgive you?
Pilgrim: Yes.
Minister: Christ have mercy.

Pilgrim: Christ have mercy.

The Minister asks if there is any other person and, if so, this is repeated person by person:

Minister: God of love, you gather all your children like a mother. Gather both _____ *(the named person)* and _____ *(the Pilgrim)* into your embrace of love everlasting.

Minister: Is there anyone who has died with whom you wish to be reconciled?

Pilgrim: Yes/No.

If the answer is 'yes', the person may be named and the Minister says:

Minister: Christ have mercy.

Pilgrim: Christ have mercy.

Minister: Jesus Christ, truly human, truly God, you are the mediator between us in both this world and the next. May your servant now be at peace with the one from whom she/he was estranged. Communicate to the one estranged all that they need to know, and give them peace, too.

Minister: Is there anything you have done, said or withheld which is on your conscience, and for which you want forgiveness?

Pilgrim: Yes/No.

Minister: Christ have mercy.

Pilgrim: Christ have mercy.

Minister: Loving God, you brought us to birth and reach out your arms to receive us into our eternal home. Forgive your servant these sins, heal her/him and those she/he leaves behind of all that disfigures them, scatter the darkness from her/his path, that she/he may journey ever nearer to you.

If this is desired, the Minister may anoint the dying person with oil on the forehead using words such as these:

Minister: I anoint you with this oil that God may inwardly anoint you with forgiveness of your sins and release from your worries. May God deliver you from all ill, fill you with goodness and lead you to everlasting life.

FORGIVENESS PARLOUR

We may have put things right as far as we can, but, being human, all kinds of thoughts can rise to the surface which accuse or torment us. It is good to have somewhere in our departure lounge which keeps the forgiving heart of God always before us.

Choose a picture or a text which does this for you.

My choice is Rembrandt's portrait *The Prodigal Son.* The son who ran away and wasted all that his parents gave him eventually returns and kneels before his father. The father neither rejects nor distances himself from him. He embraces him warmly and places his arms around his shoulders, welcoming him home.

Rembrandt here portrays Jesus' parable in which the father is an image of God, and the son is an image of each of us.

MUSIC

When I am slipping away from earth and drawing near to heaven, what sort of music would I like to hear?

From earliest times, bards were called to play music at the bedside of a person in crisis or at death's door. Or perhaps a soul friend or group of singers would chant or sing over a dying person. Such music can soothe, assure, uplift and carry the person over to the 'next shore'.

Welsh harpist Annie Mawson was singing in Welsh to a sick child in hospital when a man who was visiting his dying father asked her if she would sing in Welsh to him as he entered his last hour or two. She was happy to oblige.

On another occasion, Annie was playing the harp at the little chapel of St Cedd at Bradwell on Sea, Essex, after a great gathering at which Cardinal Basil Hume had spoken. He came in to rest because, unknown then to her, he had inoperable cancer. He said he would like her to sing for him and, knowing of his love of the Holy Island of Lindisfarne, Annie sang words by David Adam, which she entitled 'Home Thoughts from Lindisfarne':

> Lord, there are times when I need to be an island
> Set in an infinite sea
> Cut off from all that comes to me
> But surrounded still by Thee...
>
> Full tide, ebb tide
> Let life's rhythms flow
> Ebb tide, full tide
> How life's beat must go.[1]

What kind of music would you like during your last weeks or at your funeral? There are several ways of looking at this.

- We might choose whatever happens to be our current 'top of the pops'. That may be fine if we die quickly, but will we still like it when it has faded from the charts? Also, supposing we are often on a 'high', or have an addiction, will we want music that plays to these things, or music that plays to a phase in our journey which involves us being weaned onto something more eternally real?

• Often people choose a pop song from a decade which was a happy time for them. Many pop songs are about love. They express our heart's desires. As we grow weaker, the barriers which prevent us living from the love within us can seem less important.

• We might choose music that we liked at an important early stage of our life. The following story explains why this can be opportune. A regular visitor to a geriatric man in a nursing home was told one day that the old man could no longer respond to anyone. His brain and his awareness seemed already dead, even though he could breathe and eat. The visitor at first resigned herself to a lack of communication, but then she remembered that the old man had once talked about his youthful tastes. She acquired some music from that period and played it at his bedside. Gradually recognition, then movement, then limited speech returned to the old man. That music evoked memory, meaning and movement. It was truly music at midnight.

• We might choose music that has already passed the test of time for us – music that we have enjoyed over a long period.

We each focus on different aspects of life. One friend of mine focused on gratitude for the life he would soon be leaving. 'What a Wonderful World' was his choice of song. Another person focused on the world she hoped for her children. Her choice was Dvořák's *New World* symphony.

Some of us are more inclined to focus on the glory that awaits us. I think, when I am fading, that I would like the background music of Handel's 'Hallelujah Chorus', and the air that follows it:

Hallelujah: for the Lord God Omnipotent reigneth.
The kingdom of this world has become
the kingdom of our Lord, and of His Christ;
and He shall reign for ever and ever.
King of Kings, and Lord of Lords, Hallelujah!

Then comes:

I know that my Redeemer liveth,
and that He shall stand at the last day
upon the earth;
and though worms destroy this body,
yet in my flesh shall I see God.
For now is Christ risen from the dead,
the first fruits of them that sleep.

John Bell of the Wild Goose Resources Group has produced a cassette and book of beautiful music for the 'Last Journey'. It includes this song:

From the falter of breath,
through the silence of death,
to the wonder that's breaking beyond;
God has woven a way,
unapparent by day,
for all those of whom heaven is fond.

From frustration and pain,
through hope hard to sustain,
to the wholeness here promised, there known;
Christ has gone where we fear
and has vowed to be near
on the journey we make on our own.

From the dimming of light,
through the darkness of night,
to the glory of goodness above:
God the Spirit is sent
to ensure heaven's intent
is embraced and completed in love.[2]

Requiem masses have been put to music by many of the greatest composers. Living composers such as John Tavener provide music with a mystical quality. His 'Song for Athene' was sung at the funeral of Princess Diana:

Alleluia. May flights of angels sing thee to thy rest.
Remember me, O Lord, when you come into your kingdom.

Give rest, O Lord, to your handmaid, who has fallen asleep.
The choir of saints have found the wellspring of life, and door of
    paradise.
Life: a shadow and a dream.
Weeping at the grave creates the song:
Alleluia. Come, enjoy the rewards and crowns I have prepared for
    you.

If we can sing or play an instrument, there might be a final song we ourselves wish to offer.

On her CD and cassette *Angel Voices Ever Singing*, Annie Mawson includes a song called 'David of the White Rock', which imagines King David of the Bible, who played his harp to bless others when he was young, sensing that angels were calling him to play his harp once more before he died. He sang these words:

Bring me said David
The harp that I adore
I know that death calls me
to play it once more
I long to touch my beloved strings again.
On widow and children God's blessing remain.

Last night the voice of an angel did say
Come home, O David, for I hear you play
Above my youth and your music adieu
Widow and children God's blessing on you.

In the light of what I have written above, think about the music you would like before you die. Write down below the title of a song or piece of music that conjures up something familiar or loved, which you would like someone to sing or play for you when your midnight approaches.

I would like to hear this music before I depart:

PRAYERS

One way in which we can prepare for our own death is to be fully present at the death of another. The prayers you say for others can be said by others for you.

Often we long to be a help to friends or family when they near their end, but we do not know how, or fear we will 'put our foot in it'. It is good just to be present with a loved one, to hold them. This itself can be prayer. There can also be a time for spoken prayers.

In the Scottish Highlands and Islands, friends and family used to gather round a person whose strength was fading to say prayers which they called the 'soul leading' or 'soul peace'. We, too, can do this.

Blessings over a dying person may be said by a minister, relative or friend, alone or with others present. The 'soul peace' should be said slowly, and all present can join the dying person (if he or she is conscious) in asking the Three Persons of the Trinity and the saints in heaven to receive the departing soul.

During the prayer a friend may make the sign of the cross on the frail or dying person's forehead, or place a crucifix before their eyes. A well-known Bible passage, psalm or hymn may be read, even to people who have little religious background, and one or more of these prayers may be repeated from time to time.

PRAYERS TO BE SAID BY OR WITH YOU OR ON YOUR BEHALF

God be in my head, and in my understanding.
God be in my eyes, and in my looking.
God be in my mouth, and in my speaking.
God be in my heart, and in my thinking.
God be at my end, and at my departing.
TRADITIONAL

I am going home with you, to your home, to your home;
I am going home with you, to your home of mercy.
I am going home with you, to your home, to your home;
I am going home with you, to the place of all the blessings.
CARMINA GADELICA[3]

Lord, you loved me before I was born
And in your arms I die.
Take me nearer to your heart
To the place of light, and love everlasting.

Father in heaven
in weakness and in strength
I bear your likeness.
Now I am in the land of shadows
where the light of memory is dimmed.
But I am coming to you.
I shall know you as you know me.
Glory to you.
Glory to you.

As it was in the stillness of the morning
so may it be in the silence of the night.
As it was in the hidden vitality of the womb
so may it be at my birth into eternity.
As it was in the beginning, O God,
so in the end may your gift be born
so in the end may your gift of life be born.

J. PHILIP NEWELL[4]

Deep peace of the quiet earth.
Deep peace of the heavenly spheres.
Deep peace of the still waters.
Deep peace of the Son of Peace
Peace above all peace
Peace without end.

Lamb of God,
who takes away the sins of the world,
have mercy on me.
Lamb of God,
who takes away the sins of the world,
have mercy upon me.
Lamb of God,
who takes away the sins of the world,
grant me your peace.

TRADITIONAL LITURGY

Risen Christ, by your death you have destroyed death.
By your visiting the spirits of the dead
You opened to them the gate of glory.
By your resurrection you give us eternal life.
Through baptism we have been united to your death.
Raise us up to live with you in the resurrection.

Lord Jesus,
I thank you for all the benefits you have won for me,
for all the pains and insults you have borne for me.
Most merciful redeemer, friend and brother,
May I see you more clearly,
Love you more dearly,
and follow you more nearly,
day by day.
ST RICHARD OF CHICHESTER

Soul of Christ, make me holy.
Jesus, within your wounds hide me.
In the hour of my death, call me to you,
that with your saints I may love you for ever.
TRADITIONAL

Christ be near me, Christ within me
Christ beneath me, Christ above me
Christ beside me
Christ to win me
Christ to comfort and restore me.
Christ in quiet, Christ in danger
Christ in heart of friend and stranger.
FROM ST PATRICK'S BREASTPLATE (ADAPTED)

Blessed death will be welcomed by us.
Angels' music will be heard by us.
You are the Treasure I most desire.
Your face, Lord, will I seek.
Heaven's beauty I desire more than all things.

PRAYERS TO BE SAID FOR YOU AND BESIDE YOU

Tick the ones you especially like.

Merciful God
Set him/her free from the restrictions of earth
That he/she may reflect the fullness of the person you made him/her
    to be.

God be with you today and for ever.
Jesus be in you to pardon and tether.
Spirit be on you and leave you never.
May kindly Michael,
Chief of the holy angels,
Take charge of your beloved soul,
And tenderly bring it home
To the Three of limitless love,
Creator, Saviour, Eternal Life-giver.

The Three Persons of God encircle you.
The Saving Three set you free.
The loving Three caress you and work in you,
In your loved ones,
In those who have gone before you,
In your dark,
In your day,
In your pain,
In your seeing,
In your journey,
Now, for ever.
Hold those I love in your arms.
Be their strength.
Give them grace to persevere.

In the Name of the all-powerful Father,
In the Name of the all-loving Son,
In the Name of the pervading Spirit,
I command all spirit of fear to leave you,
I break the power of unforgiven sin in you,
I set you free from dependence upon human ties
That you may be as free as the wind,

As soft as sheep's wool,
As straight as an arrow,
And that you may journey into the heart of God.

Go forth upon your journey from this world,
In the Name of God the Father who created you;
In the Name of Jesus Christ who died for you;
In the Name of the Holy Spirit who shines through you;
In friendship with God's saints;
Aided by the holy angels.
May you rest this day in
the peace and love of your eternal home.

TRADITIONAL FUNERAL LITURGY (ADAPTED)

Father, I place N..... into your hands;
Acknowledge a sheep of your own fold,
A lamb of your own flock,
A sinner of your own redeeming.
Enfold N..... in the arms of your mercy.

TRADITIONAL FUNERAL LITURGY

PRAYERS AT THE VERY END

These will be personal to each individual. They will be instinctive;
they may be prayers that were stored in the soul in childhood. In my
case, I suspect my last prayers might be these:

Yesterday, today, for ever, Jesus is the same.
All may change, but Jesus never, Jesus is the same.
Jesus is the same.
Jesus is the same.
Yesterday, today, for ever, Jesus is the same.

ANON

Moment by moment I'm kept in his love.
Moment by moment I've life from above.
Looking to Jesus till glory doth shine.
Moment by moment, O Lord, I am Thine.

Thou art the Potter,
I am the clay.
Mould me and make me
In Thine own way.
Whatever the vessel,
Grant me to be
Used in Thy service to glorify Thee.

Add your own or favourite prayer below.

ANGELS

It is good to remember that God gives us angels to care for us as we move through death. Our departure lounge should have angel presences, whether through pictures, ikons, music or prayers.

My good angel, messenger of God,
Protect my body and my soul;
Protect me from the evil spirit
And above all else from sin.
I pray you, saints, men and women,
I pray you, Jesus,
To protect me and obtain for me
A good and happy death.

FROM BRITTANY[5]

May the seven angels of the Holy Spirit
And the two guardian angels
Shield me this night and every night
Till light and dawn shall come.

CARMINA GADELICA[6]

SONGS

There is a space in the pull-out form at the back of this book (see page 237) for you to state songs, hymns, music or poems you would like to listen to on your deathbed or to have at your funeral. These should reflect *your* tastes. We are each so different and our tastes differ widely. These songs, hymns and chants can be sung to you, or you can record them now so that you can play them when you want to, or they can simply be read.

The following hymn is perhaps the most popular traditional hymn in Britain (it is even sung at the English FA Cup Final).

Abide with me: fast falls the eventide;
The darkness deepens; Lord, with me abide:
When other helpers fail, and comforts flee,
Help of the helpless, O abide with me.

Swift to its close ebbs out life's little day;
Earth's joys grow dim, its glories pass away;
Change and decay in all around I see;
O Thou, who changest not, abide with me.

I need Thy presence every passing hour;
What but Thy grace can foil the tempter's power?
Who like Thyself my guide and stay can be?
Through cloud and sunshine, Lord, abide with me.

I fear no foe with Thee at hand to bless;
Ills have no weight, and tears no bitterness.
Where is death's sting? Where, grave, thy victory?
I triumph still, if Thou abide with me.

Hold Thou Thy Cross before my closing eyes;
Shine through the gloom, and point me to the skies.
Heaven's morning breaks, and earth's vain shadows flee;
In life, in death, O Lord, abide with me.

H.F. LYTE (1793–1847)

The Lord's my Shepherd, I'll not lack.
He makes me down to lie
In pastures green, and leadeth me,
The quiet waters by.
My soul He doth restore again,
And me to walk doth make
Within the paths of blessedness,
E'en for His own dear sake.

Yea, though I pass through death's dark vale,
Yet will I fear no ill,
For Thou art with me, and Thy voice
And staff me comfort still.
You bring to me such lovely things,
In presence of my woes;
You bathe my being with oil of love,
And my life overflows.

Goodness and mercy all my days
Shall surely follow me;
And in my Father's Heart always
My dwelling place shall be.

A VERSION OF PSALM 23

This hymn by G. Markland, based on Isaiah 43:1–4, provides divine comfort in time of trial.

Do not be afraid, for I have redeemed you
I have called you by my name, you are mine.

When you walk through the waters I'll be with you,
you will never sink beneath the waves.

When the fire is burning all around you,
you will never be consumed by the flames.

When the fear of loneliness is looming,
then remember I am at your side.

When you dwell in the exile of the stranger,
remember you are precious in my eyes.

You are mine, O my child, I am your Father,
and I love you with a perfect love.[7]

Breathe on me, Breath of God:
so shall I never die,
but live with thee the perfect life
of thine eternity.

THE LAST VERSE OF A HYMN BY EDWIN HATCH (1835–89)

Some people like 'golden oldie' hymns such as this verse from 'Blessed Assurance':

Perfect submission, perfect delight,
visions of rapture burst on my sight;
angels descending, bring from above
echoes of mercy, whispers of love.

This is my story, this is my song
praising my Saviour, all the day long;
this is my story, this is my song,
praising my Saviour, all the day long.

Those who are not attracted by that kind of hymn may be drawn instead by a hymn such as the following by George Matheson:

O love that wilt not let me go,
I rest my weary soul in Thee;
I give Thee back the life I owe,
that in Thine ocean depths its flow
may richer, fuller be.

O Light that followest all my way,
I yield my flickering torch to Thee;
my heart restores its borrowed ray,
that in Thy sunshine's blaze its day
may brighter, fairer be.

O Joy that seekest me through pain,
I cannot close my heart to Thee;
I trace the rainbow through the rain,

and feel the promise is not vain
that morn shall tearless be.

O Cross that liftest up my head,
I dare not ask to fly from Thee;
I lay in dust life's glory dead,
and from the ground there blossoms red
life that shall endless be.

Some people are helped by chants that are sung quietly and repeat-
edly, such as these words from the Bible which the Taizé Community
in France have put to music.

Bless the Lord, my soul
And bless God's holy name
Bless the Lord, my soul,
Who rescues me from death.

Bless the Lord, my soul
And bless God's holy name
Bless the Lord, my soul,
Who leads me into life.

FROM PSALM 103

The following chant uses the words of the thief who was dying next
to Jesus.

Jesus, remember me,
when you come into your kingdom.
Jesus, remember me,
when you come into your kingdom.

FROM LUKE 23:42

Others are helped by short choruses, so simple that a child could
repeat them. As a teenager I bound this little chorus to myself. I
included it in the selection of prayers above, and I expect to say it on
my deathbed.

Moment by moment I'm kept in his love.
Moment by moment I've life from above.
Looking to Jesus till glory shall shine.
Moment by moment, O Lord, I am thine.

POETS' CORNER

It is a good idea, while we still have strength, to create a loose-leaf book of poems which we would like to read or hear during our last journey. These could be made into a 'poets' corner' in the room to which we are confined. Since we are each made so differently, preferences will vary greatly.

I wrote the following poem on 16 February 1993 in the same room as my friend Nigel, aged 31, a month before he died.

Travelling on

You have travelled through life
from your mother's womb.
God was in your mother's womb.

You have travelled through life
into hurts and hopes.
God was in your hurts and hopes.

You have travelled through life
into loves and regrets.
God was in your loves and regrets.

You have travelled through life
into worries and work.
God was in your worries and work.

You have travelled through life
into sights and sounds.
God was in your sights and sounds.

You have travelled through life
into tempers and trials.
God was in those tempers and trials.

You have travelled through life
into frailty and loss.
God was in your frailty and loss.

You are travelling now
towards Death and Beyond.
God is with you in Death and Beyond.

I like this poem, too, sent to me by Brian Frost.

Farewell, my lovely friends,
It is time for us to part;
Farewell, farewell,
Don't grieve and wish
There had never been
A sharing of the heart.

Farewell, my lovely friends,
The end was in the start;
Farewell, farewell,
We'll take our leave
Though memories sting and smart.

Farewell, my lovely friends,
In God's good time we'll meet;
Farewell, farewell,
Don't check your tears
But remember this across the years:
In another world of bliss
We'll greet – and never be apart.

BRIAN FROST[8]

This poem is from Rainer Maria Rilke's *Book of Hours*.

God, give us each our own death,
the dying that proceeds
from each of our lives:

the way we loved,
the meanings we made,
our need.[9]

Death, thou wast once an uncouth hideous thing,
Nothing but bones,
The sad effect of sadder groans:
Thy mouth was open, but thou couldst not sing.

For we consider'd thee at some six
Or ten years hence,
After the loss of life and sense,
Flesh being turned to dust, and bones to sticks.

But since our Saviour's death did put some blood into thy face;
Thou art grown fair and full of grace...

GEORGE HERBERT (1593–1633)

Heaven-haven

I have desired to go
Where springs not fail,
To fields where flies no sharp and sided hail
And a few lilies blow
And I have asked to be
Where no storms come,
Where the green swell is in the havens dumb,
And out of the swing of the sea.

GERARD MANLEY HOPKINS (1844–99)

Since there is a poet in each of us, why not write your own poem?
This is what someone who came to our Retreat House at Lindisfarne
wrote:

When the sea comes calling

I built my house by the sea.
Not on the sands, mind you, not on the shifting sand.
And I built it of rock.
A strong house
By a strong sea.
And we got well acquainted, the sea and I.
Good neighbours.
Not that we spoke much.
We met in silences,

Respectful, keeping our distance
But looking our thoughts across the fence of sand.
Always the fence of sand our barrier,
Always the sand between.
And then one day
(And I still don't know how it happened)
The sea came.
Without warning.
Without welcome even.
Not sudden and swift, but a shifting across the sand like wine,
Less like the flow of water than the flow of blood.
Slow, but flowing like an open wound.
And I thought of flight, and I thought of drowning, and I thought
    of death.
But while I thought the sea crept higher till it reached my door.
And I knew that there was neither flight nor death nor drowning.
That when the sea comes calling you stop being good neighbours,
And you give your house for a coral castle
And you learn to breathe under water.

The late Bishop Cuthbert Bardsley gave the following words to
Francis Coulson, the co-founder of Sharrow Bay Country House
Hotel, with its legendary ethos of love. It was read at Francis's
funeral at Carlisle Cathedral.

Then into His hand went mine
Into my heart came He
I walked in the Light Divine
The path that I feared to see.

For myself, I suspect that when I am near the end I will need only
poems that speak directly to my innermost being.

Alone with none but you, my God,
I journey on my way.
What need I fear, when you are near,
O King of night and day?
More safe am I within your hand
Than if a host did round me stand.

My life I yield to your command,
And bow to your control,
In peaceful calm, for from your arm
No power can snatch my soul.
Could earthly foes ever appal
A soul that heeds the heavenly call?

ATTRIBUTED TO ST COLUMBA (521–97)

Of death

...For what is it to die but to stand naked in the wind and to melt into the sun?

And what is it to cease breathing but to free the breath from its restless tides, that it may rise and expand and seek God unencumbered?

Only when you drink from the river of silence shall you indeed sing.

And when you have reached the mountain top, then you shall begin to climb.

And when the earth shall claim your limbs, then shall you truly dance.

KAHLIL GIBRAN[10]

BIBLE READINGS

The Bible is a timeless treasure house. Words of deep comfort, hope and meaning can be drawn from its many-splendoured library of books, letters and poems. The Psalms have been the song book of all sorts and conditions of people, for they mirror the human soul at its high points and at its departing. What follows is a selection of some of my favourite Bible passages. I hope you will add your own favourites.

SHORT SENTENCES FROM THE PSALMS

One or more of these may be repeated several times between silences.

The LORD is my shepherd, I shall lack nothing.
PSALM 23:1

To you, O LORD, I lift up my soul.
PSALM 25:1

The LORD is my light and my salvation; whom then shall I fear?
PSALM 27:1

Wait for the LORD.
Be strong and he shall comfort your heart.
PSALM 27:14

LONGER PASSAGES FROM THE PSALMS

God is our refuge and strength,
A very present help in trouble.
Therefore will we not fear,
Though the earth should be removed,
Though the mountains shake in the midst of the sea...

There is a river whose streams make glad the city of God,
The holy dwelling of the Most High.
God is in the midst of that city.
It shall not be moved.
God will help it when the morning dawns.
Nations are in turmoil, kingdoms totter,
God utters his voice, the earth melts.
The LORD of hosts is with us.
The God of Jacob is our refuge…

Be still and know that I am God.
I will be exalted among the nations,
I will be exalted in the earth.
The LORD of hosts is with us.
The God of Jacob is our refuge.
FROM PSALM 46

As a deer longs for the flowing streams
so my soul longs for you, O God.
My soul thirsts for God,
for the living God.
When shall I come and behold the face of God?
My tears have been my food day and night,
while people say to me continually,
'Where is your God?'

…Why are you cast down, O my soul,
and why are you disquieted within me?
Hope in God;
for I shall again praise the One who is my help and my God.
FROM PSALM 42

You who live in the shelter of the Most High,
who abide in the shadow of the Almighty,
will say to God, 'My refuge and my fortress;
my God, in whom I trust.'

...Because you have made God your refuge,
the Most High your dwelling place,
no evil shall befall you,
no scourge shall come near your tent.

For God will command angels concerning you,
to guard you in all your ways...

Those who love me, I will deliver;
I will protect those who know my name.
When they call to me, I will answer them;
I will be with them in trouble.

FROM PSALM 91

Bless the LORD, O my soul,
and all that is within me bless God's holy name.
Bless the LORD, O my soul,
and forget not all God's benefits –
who forgives your iniquity,
who heals your diseases,
who redeems your life from the pit,
who crowns you with steadfast love and mercy...

As for mortals, their days are as grass;
they flourish like a flower of the field;
for the wind passes over it, and it is gone,
and the place knows it no more.
But the steadfast love of the LORD is from everlasting to everlasting
on those who revere God,
and God's righteousness to children's children,
to those who keep covenant
and remember to do God's commands.

God has established a throne in the heavens,
and God's dominion rules over all.
Bless the LORD, you angels,
you mighty ones, who do God's bidding...
Bless the LORD, all you hosts,
you ministers who do God's will.
Bless the LORD, all the works of the LORD

in all places of God's dominion.
Bless the LORD, O my soul.

FROM PSALM 103

I lift up my eyes to the hills.
From where will my help come?
My help comes from God,
who made heaven and earth.
God will not let your foot be moved;
the One who keeps you will not slumber.
The One who keeps Israel will neither slumber nor sleep.

God is your keeper;
God is your shade at your side.
The sun shall not strike you by day,
nor the moon by night.
God will keep you from all evil,
and will keep your life.
God will keep your going out and your coming in
from this time on and for evermore.

PSALM 121

SHORT SENTENCES FROM OTHER PARTS OF SCRIPTURE

One or more of these may be repeated several times between silences.

The eternal God is your dwelling place,
and underneath are the everlasting arms.

DEUTERONOMY 33:27

When I felt my life slipping away,
then, O Lord, I prayed to you,
and in your holy Temple you heard me.

JONAH 2:7

The steadfast love of the LORD never ceases,
whose mercies never come to an end.

LAMENTATIONS 3:22

Jesus said, 'I am with you always, even to the end of the age.'
MATTHEW 28:20

The Lord Jesus said, 'Today you will be with me in Paradise.'
LUKE 23:43

God loved the world so much that he gave his only Son, that whoever trusts in him should not die, but should have everlasting life. JOHN 3:16

Jesus said, 'I will raise up on the last day all who believe in the Son.' JOHN 6:40

Jesus said, 'I am the resurrection and the life. Those who believe in me, even though they die, will live.' JOHN 11:25

Where my Father lives there are many living quarters. JOHN 14:2

I go to prepare a place for you. And I will come again and take you to myself, so that where I am, there you may be also.
JOHN 14:3

Lord Jesus, receive my spirit. ACTS 7:59

Neither death nor life ... nor anything in heaven or earth will be able to separate us from the love of God in Christ Jesus our Lord.
ROMANS 8:38,39

Christ died and lived again, so that he might be Lord of both the dead and the living. ROMANS 14:9

Love is eternal ... Three things last: faith, hope, and love, but the greatest of these is love. I CORINTHIANS 13:8,13

Now we see in a mirror dimly, but the time will come when we shall see face to face. I CORINTHIANS 13:12

We know that we have a building from God, a house not made with hands, eternal in the heavens ... We are always full of courage. We know that as long as we are at home in this body we are away from the Lord. 2 CORINTHIANS 5:1,6

We will be with the Lord for ever. 1 THESSALONIANS 4:17

We will see God as he is. 1 JOHN 3:2

OTHER PASSAGES FROM SCRIPTURE

At sunset Jacob came to a holy place and camped there. He lay down to sleep, resting his head on a stone. He dreamed that he saw a ladder reaching from earth to heaven, with angels going up and coming down on it. And the LORD was standing beside him ... Jacob woke up and said, 'The LORD is here ... this must be the gate that opens into heaven.' GENESIS 28:10-13,16,17

'Do not be worried and upset,' Jesus told them. 'Believe in God and believe also in me. There are many rooms in my Father's house, and I am going to prepare a place for you. I would not tell you this if it were not so. And after I go and prepare a place for you, I will come back and take you to myself, so that you will be where I am.' JOHN 14:1-3

How are the dead raised? ... The seed you sow does not come to life unless it has first died. What you sow is not the body that shall be, but a naked grain, of wheat or some other kind; and God clothes it with the body of his choice, each seed with its own particular body. It is like that with the resurrection of the dead. What is sown in the earth is a perishable thing: it is raised imperishable ... It is sown in weakness: it is raised in power. It is sown an animal body: it is raised a spiritual body ... When our mortality has been clothed with immortality, then the saying of Scripture will come true: 'Death is swallowed up in victory' ... The sting of death is sin, but God gives us the victory through our Lord Jesus Christ. SELECTED VERSES FROM 1 CORINTHIANS 15

I saw a new heaven and a new earth ... I heard a loud voice speaking from the throne: 'Now God's home is with human beings. God will live with them and will be their God. God will wipe all tears from their eyes. There will be no more death, no more grief or crying or pain.' REVELATION 21:1,3,4

FAVOURITE BIBLE VERSES

If you, or someone you ask, knows a favourite Bible verse, write it down here.

THINGS TO LOOK AT

- A favourite picture can be taken from its usual place and hung in the room where you lie.
- A photograph can be placed where you can see it easily.
- Those who find ikons helpful might choose one that points them to eternal certainties. I love the ikon of Christ descending into hell after his resurrection to rescue the spirits trapped there.
- Something beautiful should be near to us – flowers, a carving, something from creation, a designed cloth.
- Albums, drawings, flowers and letters from grandchildren and others will bless us.

* * *

Why not write down the things you would like to look at?

I would like to look at:

SOMETHING TO HOLD

We may become too weak to speak or think much, but we can always hold on to something in our hand, up to and beyond our last breath.

To hold another human hand can be a beautiful thing. 'Your hand is so gentle it could hold a bird,' a dying person told a friend.

A human hand is not always available, however. Some people might hold a memento, a cuddly toy, or an object of religious significance.

In the days when Britain imposed a death penalty on some criminals, Strangeways Prison had a death wing. No human hand was there. Only two things were allowed in the room where convicts awaited their death – a Bible and a cross with the dying Christ carved on it. Over the years, the head of Christ wore away. Before they went to their death, many inmates took hold of Christ's head and held it to them with all their strength.

One of the most popular items produced by the wood workshops at Bowthorpe, Norwich, are 'holding crosses'." They are designed to feel right rather than to look right. The cross beam is deliberately uneven, in order to fit between fingers more comfortably than a 'correctly' shaped cross would. Because a holding cross is not decorated or ornamental, it is a true reminder of the harsh wood of the cross of Jesus.

Sometimes it is enough for us simply to hold the cross silently – we express our love or need of Christ through our sense of touch. Sometimes a few simple or familiar words may help.

As I hang on to this cross,
Lord, hang on to me.

You are in this hell with me.
You are Love-in-Death.

Lord, I believe.
Help my unbelief.

Your cross my sure way from earth to heaven.

Christ has died.
Christ is risen.
Christ will come again!

DIARIES, ALBUMS AND VIDEOS

We are each so different. We should do what we are comfortable with. The following suggestions may be right for some people and not for others.

- If you have written a diary, or a journal, or simply the 'milestones' of your life as suggested earlier in this book, why not keep this near you? Then visitors or carers can read to you from it.
- You may have recorded a diary, in which case the tapes can be played.
- You may wish to have photograph albums to hand.
- You or others may have videos showing highlights of your life – a wedding, birthday, holiday, perhaps. Or you may have a video of a place that has been a physical or spiritual home to you.

A PRIVATE PLACE

A dying person needs to increase detachment from the bonds formed in this life. That is why some dying people ask that close family should not be with them at death. The family should not be upset by this, for it shows that the dying person recognizes the strength of those bonds.

Those who are close to the dying person may cry, or in other ways activate those bonds. Hugs and tears are better shared before the very end.

A chaplain or soul friend who focuses on God more than on past attachments may be more helpful at the very end than one who is grieving so much that they cannot bear to let go.

The departure lounge, therefore, should have an exit door with this notice over it: 'No attachments.'

LITURGY FOR THE GREAT PASSAGE

Resignation to the fact of death can take a positive or a negative form. It can be hopeless, like losing a race and burying yourself. Or it can be a positive turning towards what comes after death. People are helped to turn in this positive direction in various ways. Here are two of them:

- By repeating a 'soul phrase' over and again, such as the phrase, 'Receive my soul.'
- By holding or looking at a cross or ikon.

For me, no departure lounge would be complete without a Liturgy for The Great Passage. The following liturgy, drawn from the Orthodox Church, may be said or sung at the funeral, or at another time at church or at home. I would like it read (and I ask my friends to please note this) just before and after I finally lose consciousness.

THE LITANY

If the Priest is male, the Reader(s) should be female, and vice versa. The part of the Reader(s) may be sung. The Voice represents the deceased.

Priest: Blessed be God, now and for ever, world without end. Amen.
Reader(s): Blessed are those who are undefiled and who walk in the law of the Lord. Give rest, O Lord, to the soul of your servant. Remember, O Lord, the soul of your servant.
Voice: Let my soul live and it shall praise you. I have strayed like a lost sheep. O seek your servant, for I do not forget your commands. Blessed are you, Lord; teach me your statutes. I am an image of your eternal glory; though I bear the marks of sin, show compassion towards me. Purify me by your loving kindness. Bring me to the homecoming which is my heart's desire, making me again a citizen of paradise. The departed saints have found the fountain of life and the door of paradise. May I also find the right way through repentance. I am the lost sheep. Call me, O Saviour, and save me.

Reader(s): Give rest, O Lord, to the soul of your servant, and establish him/her in paradise where the saints and those made right with you shine like the stars of heaven. Give rest to your servant who has fallen asleep; regard not his/her transgressions. Glory to the Father and to the Son and to the Holy Spirit now and for ever and world without end. Amen.

Priest: Again and again let us pray to the Lord. Lord, have mercy. Have mercy on the soul of your servant now departed and grant him/her rest and forgiveness for all his/her sins. For the mercy of God, for the kingdom of heaven, O Christ our immortal king and God, release him/her from his/her sins, we beseech you.

All: Amen.

Voice: Beholding the sea of life surging with the flood of temptations, I run to the calm haven and cry to you: raise my life from corruption, O Most Merciful One.

Reader(s): With the saints give rest, O Christ, to the soul of your servant, where there is neither sickness, nor sighing, nor sorrow, but life everlasting. You alone are immortal, who created and fashioned humankind. For out of the earth were we mortals made, and to the earth shall we return. Glory to you, Lord, glory to you, now and through the ages. Amen. Give rest, O Lord, to the soul of your servant. I weep when I think upon death, and behold our beauty, fashioned after the image of God, lying in the tomb disfigured, dishonoured, bereft of form. O marvel! What is the mystery which befalls us? Why have we been given over to corruption? Why have we been wedded to death? In truth it is by the command of God who gives the departed rest. O happy fault, that through decay and death comes life more glorious than mere mortals can conceive. Glory to the Father, glory to the Son, glory to the Holy Spirit now and through the ages for ever and ever. Amen.

Priest: Remember us, Lord, when you come into your kingdom. Blessed are the poor in spirit, for theirs is the kingdom of heaven. Blessed are they who mourn, for they shall be comforted. Blessed are the meek, for they shall inherit the earth. O Christ, who declared the thief on the cross who cried to you, 'Remember me,' to be a citizen of paradise, make me, a sinner, worthy of the same.

You who rule our souls and bodies, in whose hand is our breath, give rest to your servant whom you have taken from us.

Christ give you rest in the land of the living and open to you the gates of paradise, and make you a citizen of the kingdom of heaven, and remit all your sins, O you lover of Christ. Blessed are you when you are persecuted and when people say all manner of things against you. Rejoice! Be exceeding glad, for great is your reward in heaven.

There may be readings from 1 Thessalonians 4:13–18 and from John 5:24–30, and the Lord's Prayer.

Reader(s): O pure and holy Virgin who without seed bore God, pray to him that the soul of his servant may be saved. O holy saints of God (the saints may be named), pray to the Lord to receive his/her soul in glory.

Priest: O God of all spirits and all flesh, who has trampled down Death, and overthrown the Devil, and given life to the world; may you, the same God, give rest to the soul of your departed servant in a place of light, of fulfilment, of rest, whence sorrow and sickness and sighing have fled. Pardon every transgression, for there is no one on earth who has not sinned, and you are the all-Compassionate One. You are a good God and you love humankind. You are the Resurrection, and the Life, and the Repose of your departed servant.

Reader(s): Glory to the Father and to the Son and to the Holy Spirit now and for ever and world without end. Amen.

Priest: May the One who has power over the living and the dead, who himself rose from the dead, Christ our very God, through the prayers of his all-pure mother and of his holy saints, establish in the dwellings of the righteous his servant who has been taken from us, give him/her rest in the bosom of Abraham's family, number him/her among those made righteous, and have mercy on us all, for he is good and kind and loves all people.

All: Amen.

Reader(s): Eternal remembrance. Eternal remembrance.

Saints. Angels. Eternal remembrance.

We who remain on earth. Eternal remembrance.

All: Amen.

There may be music or singing.

PART FIVE

* * *

THE OTHER SIDE

In death will be opened up all the wonder and
the joy, the love and the laughter of eternity.

THE LONG JUMP

'The Flying Rodleighs are trapeze artists who perform in the German Circus Simoneit-Barum,' the leader of the troupe once told Henri Nouwen. 'As a flyer, I must have complete trust in my catcher. The public might think that I am the great star of the trapeze, but the real star is Joe, my catcher. He has to be there for me with split-second precision and grab me out of the air as I come to him in the long jump.'

'How does it work?' Nouwen asked.

'The secret,' Rodleigh replied, 'is that the flyer does nothing and the catcher does everything. When I fly to Joe, I have simply to stretch out my arms and hands and wait for him to catch me and pull me to safety over the apron behind the catch bar.'

In his book *Our Greatest Gift*, Henri Nouwen goes on to relate his reaction to Rodleigh's statement:

'You do nothing!' I said, surprised.

'Nothing,' Rodleigh repeated. 'The worst thing the flyer can do is to try to catch the catcher. I am not supposed to catch Joe. It's Joe's task to catch me. If I grabbed Joe's wrists, I might break them, or he might break mine, and that would be the end for both of us.'

When Rodleigh said this with so much conviction, the words of Jesus flashed into my mind: 'Father into your hands I commend my spirit.' Dying is trusting in the catcher. To care for the dying is to say, 'Don't be afraid. Remember that you are a beloved child of God. He will be there when you make your long jump. Don't try to grab him; he will grab you. Just stretch out your hands and trust, trust, trust.'[1]

Death surrenders us completely to God, it makes us pass into God. In return we have to surrender ourselves to it ... since, when death comes to us, there is nothing further for us to do but let ourselves be entirely dominated and led onwards by God.

TEILHARD DE CHARDIN[2]

Life being what it is in our world, the onset of death is often the first taste a person gets of freedom. At last the imagination can come into its own, and as a person yields to it their emotions take on surprising depth and intensity.   EDWARD F. MURPHY

GONE WHERE?

I am standing on the seashore.
A ship in the bay hits anchor,
spreads her white sails to the morning breeze
and starts out upon the ocean.

She is an object of beauty and strength,
and I stand and watch until she hangs
like a speck of white cloud
just where the sea and sky mingle with each other.

Then someone at my side says,
'There, she's gone!'
Gone where?
Gone from sight, that is all.

Just at that moment there are other eyes
watching her coming
and other souls taking up the glad shout,
'There, she's coming!'

And that is dying.

ANONYMOUS

LIFE IS JUST BEGINNING

Leaving the cemetery, some of the family were sobbing: 'All is finished.'

Others were sniffling: 'Come, come, my dear, courage, it's finished!'

Some friends murmured: 'Poor man, that's how we'll all finish.'

And others sighed in relief: 'Well, it's over.'

And I was thinking that everything was just beginning.

Yes, he had finished the last rehearsal, but the eternal show was just beginning.

The years of training were over, but the eternal work was about to commence.

He had just been born to life,

The real life,

Life that's going to last,

Life eternal.

As if there were dead people!

There are no dead people, Lord.

There are only the living, on earth and beyond.

Death is real, Lord,

But it's nothing but a moment,

A second, a step,

The step from provisional to permanent,

From temporal to eternal.

So in the death of the child the adolescent is born, from the caterpillar emerges the butterfly, from the grain the full-blown ear. MICHEL QUOIST[3]

WHEN THE SAINTS GO MARCHING IN

A famous English football team is nicknamed 'The Saints'. At their matches the crowds sing, 'O when the saints, O when the saints, O when the saints go marching in, I'll be there with them, when the saints go marching in.'

This reminds me of the funeral of my friend John Peet, who was the first founder of my Community to go to heaven.[4] Before she read a passage from the Bible, our friend Carol announced, 'John has changed his address.' As we walked out of the church into the churchyard, the organ almost got us marching as it sounded out the music for 'When the Saints Go Marching In'. John's widow Jacqui chose it because it was just the sort of thing John relished. He refused to be downhearted. He always went forward, and now he was leading us forward. As his body was lowered into the grave, I threw onto his coffin a cross which members of the Community wear. To me, he was leading what would one day become a procession of Community members into their eternal work in heaven.

Most people are not in a Community exactly like ours – but think of the crowds singing 'When the Saints Go Marching In'. Everyone belongs to a group, a family or a community of some kind.

* * *

If someone in your community asked you, 'What would you like me to throw onto your coffin when you go marching in?' what would your answer be? Think about this, and note down your wishes below.

I would like any of these things to be placed on my coffin:

THE PLACE OF RESURRECTION

The Irish have a wonderful phrase: 'your place of resurrection'. The idea is that we let our feet follow our heart, and we keep walking until we find our very own place of resurrection.

What is this place of resurrection?

It is the place where the deepest part of our being feels it belongs. It is a place where our natural surroundings, our work and our relationships flow together in a harmony of fulfilment.

The place of resurrection is also a bridge between this life and the next. For Irish saints it was important that their bodies were laid to rest in their place of resurrection, because they believed that their eternal work would be related to that place.

Thus the 93-year-old St Brendan, who died in his sister's arms away from his Clonfert home, made them promise to take his body back for burial at Clonfert, which he believed was his place of resurrection.

Saints such as Brendan understood that their work in their eternal home would relate to their earthly home. They announced that after their death they would be praying for the folk they had left behind in their place of resurrection.

This raises questions in our own age of air and space travel. Staff involved in the USA's space probe to Mars, for example, have to decide whether an astronaut who dies in space is sent spinning through space for aeons, or is brought back to earth. If there is a relationship between the soul and its temporary physical framework, does it not create disharmony to treat a body in such a way that it stays outside that framework? The psychologist C.G. Jung certainly believed this, and he believed that the soul needed time to catch up with the body during long air flights.

God may call some people to minister to areas beyond earth. There may be places of resurrection in the future that we now but dimly imagine. In our mobile society, our 'place' may be set in the context of relationships rather than territory.

Have you a place of resurrection? Where do you feel the deepest part of you belongs?

Start to pray for people in your place of resurrection as if you were praying for them from the other side. See what a difference this makes!

A VEIL THIN AS GOSSAMER

Thus shall they have communion with Thee
and, in Thee, with their beloved.
Thus shall they come to know,
in themselves, that there is no death
and that only a veil divides, thin as gossamer.

GEORGE MCLEOD[5]

Most of us at times long to communicate with loved ones who have died. If we keep the lid on this desire, we store up trouble for ourselves. We need to reconnect with the world of the dead, yet many who try to do this through occult channellers end up feeling confused or let down. A far better way is frequently to visualize the next world – although any picture is a mere glimpse of this great mystery.

Heaven has been pictured as all of these things:

- A great but intimate meal.
- A community of love, light and order.
- A place flowing with creativity and music.

In each of these pictures the Source and Lover of Life is in the centre, like the hub of a living wheel to whom everyone relates.

With this kind of understanding, we can echo prayers like this by George McLeod, the last part of which was quoted above.

Be Thou, Triune God, in the midst of us
as we give thanks for those who have gone
from the sight of earthly eyes.
They, in Thy nearer presence,
still worship with us in the mystery
of the one family in heaven and earth...
If it be Thy holy will, tell them how we love them,
and how we miss them,
and how we long for the day when we shall meet with them
again.[6]

THE MORNING AFTER

This book is entitled *Before We Say Goodbye*, but what happens *after* we say goodbye? What happens after we have made the long jump? For years I have struggled with this. In fact, it was only while preparing this book that some things about the other side began to fall into place.

For a long time I made a big mistake. I deceived myself that this life on earth is the real life, and the next life is unreal, ephemeral. Now I am sure it is the other way round. Life on earth is but a short-term laboratory with built-in obsolescence. It is an intimation of what is to come. It is like the cover of a book, the first chapter of which has yet to begin.

Yet our life on earth *is* related to the next one. It is a warm-up before the real race begins. What we do here affects what happens to us there. This life is like looking at a reflection of a glorious landscape in a faded mirror. The next life is the actual landscape. Paul, who became Christ's apostle after encountering him after his death and resurrection, described it in a similar way in his first letter to the Christians in Corinth. Before that, the great philosopher Plato explained that all the forms of this universe are but copies, or images, of eternal realities.

C.S. Lewis, the author of the Narnia series of children's stories, describes life on earth (Narnia) as 'Shadowlands'. When we look back on our life on earth from the other side, it will seem to have been like our shadow. In the final book of the Narnia series, *The Last Battle*, the children and animals go through a door to a new world. The King of All (the lion Aslan) eventually folds up the earth and the stars, as if he is taking an orange in his hand and squeezing it dry. The arriving children have been told they must leave Narnia behind for ever, but then someone explains to them that the Narnia they have left behind was not the real Narnia. That was only a shadow of what has always been here and always will be. All of the old Narnia that mattered has been drawn into the real Narnia, but it is different because it is eternally real, sharper, deeper, more wonderful. Then the Lion King tells them, 'The dream is ended: this is the morning.'[7]

Make your own imaginary journey from Shadowlands (life on earth) to the Real World.

OUT OF THE BODY EXPERIENCES

The sensation of being out of the body is a widespread human experience. A 1982 Gallup poll in the USA found that 8 million Americans claimed to have had such an experience.

There is now a sizeable body of research into near-death experiences, and an International Association for Near-Death Studies. A growing number of people who have been pronounced dead have come back to life and reported sights, sounds and sensations on a different plane of reality from anything they have previously experienced. These descriptions use words and imagery which come from each individual's experience, but there is a remarkable convergence of imagery, whatever the background of the individual.

As far as I know, the first record of someone who was pronounced to be dead and whose spirit re-entered the corpse is that of Drithelm, a seventh-century Northumbrian man. His experience is recorded by Bede.[8]

A man of shining countenance took Drithelm towards a place like a summer solstice sunrise. They saw a deep valley. A fire raged on one side, and a blizzard of icy snow raged on the other side. Wretched souls were being tossed from side to side. He later learned that these were people who had lived selfish lives, and needed to be purified before they were ready to reach their final destination. Then he was taken to a plain which was filled with happy, young-at-heart people. These were people who had been good to others on earth, but who needed to develop their character further before they were ready to move into their final destination. Drithelm became aware of a place of light in the distance where there was some wonderful singing. His guide told him this was heaven. Drithelm himself, however, was told he must return to earth. His spirit then re-entered his body.

LIFE AFTER LIFE

In the 1960s the American Dr Raymond Moody published the results of his investigations into near-death experiences in his bestseller *Life after Life*. He states, 'The disembodied spirit soon discovers the ability to travel just by willing itself to go to another location. The form of the spirit body varies and may change as the experience unfolds.'[9]

The research published in October 2000 by two British doctors, Peter Fenwick and Sam Parnia, goes further. The brains of the people in their research were officially declared to be dead. They reach the conclusion that the distinction drawn by the ancient world between the brain (*animus*) and the soul (*anima*) is indeed valid. Descartes abolished that distinction in his famous dictum, '*Cogito ergo sum*' ('I think, therefore I am'), which implies that when the brain is dead I cease to exist. One of the doctors illustrates their conclusion by likening the *anima* to television waves, which exist in their own right, quite apart from any television set. The television waves do not cease to exist when the television is turned off or removed.

Christians who have had near-death experiences are in great demand. Their stories increase our awareness that this life is but a pale shadow of that which is to come, and our human loves are but tiny hints of the Unconditional Love that prevails in heaven.

The most detailed and insightful encounter with 'the other side' known to me is that of Betty Eadie.[10] The doctors declared her to be dead after an operation. She saw her corpse, and everything she had ever felt or done in her life flashed through her mind. A mass of black energy transported her what seemed like light years away, yet she had peace, and thought 'this must be the shadow of death'. She rushed through a black tunnel towards a distant pinprick of light that grew ever nearer. The light became more brilliant than the sun. Out of this unapproachable light stepped a figure of light who embraced her, and she was filled with utter unconditional love. She somehow knew that she had always been a part of 'him' and that she was 'home'.

Endless questions tumbled out of Eadie, and she understood secrets of the ages, most of which she could not express in human words. She understood that the creative thoughts we have on earth are the result of unseen inspiration; that we are on earth for growth; that earth is not our real home, only a temporary dwelling place. She realized that everything in the material world is created by spiritual power; that living according to the laws of spiritual power causes blessing, and vice versa. She saw that all experience, whether we call it good or bad, is for our growth, including our death.

She met all sorts of spirit people, and discovered that people were working there, and that there was 'a library of the mind'. Escorts took her to a garden, and she was astonished to find that the contours and wonders of earth were also there, but they were far brighter and more real and indestructible. There was 'a new earth' in heaven. She knew that every created thing, even a microscopic plant, had its own unique 'intelligence, colour and sound, infinitely more resonant, deep, meaningful, distinct than anything on earth'.

Her memory was opened up, so that she seemed to recall things from the beginning of the world. There was vastness – many worlds – and speed and communication that knew no boundaries. Yet throughout this astral travel she felt God's love and knew that she was somehow back in her native environment. In her travels, she noticed that people were progressing, becoming more like their Father. There were many spirits, some of whom were allowed to visit earth for varying lengths of time.

Then the heavens scrolled back and she saw earth again. She zoomed in on a drunk on a sidewalk. 'Who do you see?' asked her spirit guide. They revealed to her the real spirit of this man: he was magnificent, full of light, and admired in heaven. She learned about the heavenly worth of each soul, and how every prayer is heard.

Eadie was summoned before a review body, and every detail of her life was brought under scrutiny. She condemned herself. The Saviour stepped in, however, and she understood that the review was wholly positive. Love remained throughout.

Betty Eadie was told that her work on earth was not done – but *she* had to make the choice to return. She wanted to stay. The Saviour talked her through the real issues, and then she realized that to live in love and do what is right was the same thing as being willing to return to earth.

So she returned, and her spirit re-entered her body. She lived to tell the tale.

WHAT IS THE OTHER WORLD LIKE?

I am not afraid to die. For in death will be opened up all the wonder and the joy, the love and the laughter of eternity. We shall be living in full the life we have now (but are so often too blind or selfish or lazy to see and enjoy) ... that all may share the fullness of the Risen Lord. HILARY BEASLEY[11]

Hilary Beasley's insight reveals what this phrase in the Christian Creed really means: 'I believe in the resurrection of the body.' The 'body' here refers to the spiritual body, the inalienable and essential features of the God-given personality that surmount and are trans-figured at the discarding of the physical body at death.[12]

Each person has a unique essence which is offered its own space in which to flower to the full. There is no dull uniformity, but mag-nificent variety and choice. Time, space and size do not seem to matter. No one is masked by a marred body or twisted mind. Each person is seen in his or her pristine nobility.

On earth the chemistry that draws mortals to certain others seems to be an expedient to enable deep rapport. Where there are resurrected bodies the rapport is deeper and more spontaneous – and does not need chemicals to induce it.

Relationships there will be untangled. The loving core at the heart of every true earth relationship is set free, flooding with the fullness which had hardly begun to flow on earth. The all-outness which on earth requires competition to achieve is in heaven blended with delight in the other person flowing in their potential – some-thing which on earth competition often prevents. The wonders of what we call nature are all there, but not confined by the manner in which physical elements were ordered on earth.

In heaven there is something that exactly suits every temperament and type of person. This seems to be what Jesus was getting at when he assured his friends shortly before he died, 'In my Father's house there are many places to visit. If this were not so, would I have told you that I go ahead to prepare a place for you?' (John 14:2) Jesus likens heaven to the refreshment and accommodation stops which were pro-vided for travellers on a journey. There are places to suit every person.

If the best experiences of this world are but faint intimations of what is possible in the next world, let us use this world as a place that provides us with pointers to the nature of eternal reality.

Here is a heavenly doodle:

Heaven is like:
The deep peace of the still waters
The sparkle of the stars
The flow of creativity
The fellowship of the party
The ecstasy of orgasm
The freedom of flight
The stability of rock
The communication of the information highway

* * *

Now add your own intuitions.

Heaven is like:

WHAT HAPPENS AFTER DEATH?

Ancient societies were more familiar than we are with the world of the dead, which often featured in their sleeping and waking dreams. *The Tibetan Book of the Dead* is perhaps the most famous and detailed charting of the soul's supposed migration after death. Pagan Celtic societies were also familiar with the 'other world', and Caitlin Matthews' *The Celtic Book of the Dead* is a modern attempt to rehabilitate such familiarity.[13] Many people intuit that some element of a person's essence does survive death. In Tibetan Buddhism this element enters the universal essence, or 'Mind', and thus loses memory of the personality it incarnated on earth. It may be reincarnated in another being. This will be for better or worse, according to the choices it made in this life and the peace with which it departed from it.

There is, of course, another quite different view of what happens after physical death. This is the Christian belief sometimes known as 'the resurrection of the body'. This belief accepts the possibility that the dissolution of body and mind at death is complete – but it also holds out the possibility that our personality can be resurrected in a non-physical form which nevertheless expresses its unique features as originally given by God. This path – resurrection rather than dissolution – has to be *chosen*. If it is chosen, the resurrected personality can continue to develop, but it will always remain the same personality.

How can there be both choice and continuation of our journey after death? The following illustration may throw some light on this.

Sometimes a large bus station is called a 'terminus'. That is because each bus terminates its journey there. The bus passenger's journey, however, does not terminate there. Each passenger starts a new journey, for better or worse, by foot or other form of transport, to the door of the place where they will stop next.

This will be a good – although sometimes hard – journey, if the traveller is heading for his or her God-given destination. It will be a bad and ultimately useless journey if the traveller is running away from something, or using people for his or her own ends, or just killing time.

Do any of us completely do all that we are meant to? Not completely, but if we admit our weakness and ask that, when we fail, God will carry us along the right road, then all will be well.

This teaching about a choice of journeys refers to 'heaven' and 'hell' in older Christian language.

IMAGES OF HEAVEN

Jesus spoke much in parables. A parable has been defined as an earthly story with heavenly meaning. To understand a parable, as distinct from an allegory, you have to look for the main point rather than allow yourself to be sidetracked by the details.

Here are three images of heaven which Jesus gave us.

HEAVEN IS LIKE A PARTY

Jesus spoke of heaven as being like a great wedding feast (see Matthew 22:1–14). The image of the meal points beyond itself to other features: celebration, friendship, nourishment, communication, reconnection with valued forebears, welcome for people of different backgrounds.

HEAVEN IS LIKE A COMMUNITY

Jesus chose 12 members of his 'first team' and told them that, because they had stood by him on earth, in the world to come they would have a place at his table and a prized sphere of responsibility. They would be responsible for the people groups that made up their country (see Luke 22:28–30). Their country was Israel, but the early Christians taught that Christ had brought in a 'new Israel' consisting of people of all races who do God's will (see Galations 6:16). No doubt this was based on Jesus' teaching such as that given in Matthew 8:11–12.

So heaven consists of a vast human family, but not an amorphous one. There are spheres of responsibility. We will each be given responsibilities according to the measure of our gifting and faithfulness on earth. Thus someone who learned on earth to be faithful in something practical, like finance, would be given responsibility for things that have lasting value in heaven (see Luke 16:1–12).

HEAVEN IS LIKE A RENEWED CITY

The visions Christ gave to John while he was exiled on Patmos Island included one of heaven as a 'new Jerusalem' (Revelation 21:2).

The capital city was thought of as a meeting point, which carried the aspirations of all the people. It was also compact, so that every part of the city fitted well into the rest. The people were asked to pray for it to be a city of *shalom* – harmony between people, the environment and God.

Unfortunately, it fell short of this ideal in practice. Nonetheless, by imagining heaven as a new Jerusalem, we are given a sense of heaven being a living, pulsing, harmonious 'place'. Heaven is intimate but not claustrophobic. It is free of prejudice and fulfilling.

There is one other image of heaven we would do well to bear in mind:

HEAVEN IS LIKE A RENEWED EARTH

It is not for nothing that we live out our mortal training school for eternity against the background of the earth. Although the stars that the Creator flung into space and the earth that he prepared for us here will vanish like a puff of smoke, that is not because they have no meaning for eternity. Just as our physical bodies perish, yet our eternal beings bear some relationship to them, so it is with the earth. The sustenance, solidity, fertility, fragrances, beauty and sounds of earth, sea and sky will feature in a way that will make the present creation seem like an artist's preparatory sketch. This is borne out, not only by the Scriptures, but also by the experiences of people who have died and had a peep into what is beyond.

THE ETERNAL STRUGGLE OF LOVE

There is one other image of heaven in the Bible which is all-important. This is the image of eternal struggle.

On earth the price of liberty is eternal vigilance. The story of human beings on earth is the story of endless struggles between good and evil. The graph of human good and human greed goes up and down through history.

In heaven, bodiless beings who were not vigilant fell into bad ways. These beings are variously named as demons, fallen angels, Lucifer, the Devil and Satan. The implication is that eternal vigilance is required in heaven, as on earth. To be vigilant requires effort, choice, thought, and being fully present to God.

One of the visions Jesus gave to John refers to war in heaven, when Michael, a leading angel, led the spiritual powers to victory over those who were trying to destroy good in Israel (see Revelation 12:7; also Daniel 10). There is in heaven a rider whose name is Faithful and True, whom the armies of heaven follow (see Revelation 19:11–16). The purpose of the armies is to bring everyone and everything into a relationship of love with the Trinity, the three eternal loves in the heart of God. Thus we are given the image of heaven as a marriage of the Lamb (the sacrificial, vulnerable, woundable love of God as revealed in Christ) to us humans, who are described collectively as 'the bride'.

In heaven I will wage the ceaseless 'war' of love. Of course, we think of war as requiring an enemy to hate and destroy. In heaven's war of love, we hate only what is not love – we draw all into a hate-free, fear-free, prejudice-free, greed-free and love-filled world.

Heaven is that love so great that nothing can overcome it, nothing can flourish that is not part of it, and only within it can the greatest creativity, individual fulfilment and communal harmony be combined.

THE VOYAGE TO THE OTHER SIDE

I am old ... I am like a man on a sea voyage nearing his destination. When I embarked I worried about having a cabin with a porthole, whether I should be asked to sit at the Captain's table, who were the more attractive and important passengers. All such considerations become pointless when I shall so soon be disembarking. As I do not believe that earthly life can bring any lasting satisfaction, the prospect of death holds no terrors. Those saints who pronounced themselves in love with death displayed, I consider, the best of sense. MALCOLM MUGGERIDGE[14]

The crossing from this world to the next is often likened to a sea voyage. The sea is vast and largely unknown, the vessel is frail, yet there is mystery and meaning in the voyage. I wrote the following Liturgy of the Voyage after discovering a similar one in a file, which had no attribution.

Jesus
My peace I leave with you.
Let not your hearts be troubled or afraid.

Departing soul
From the darkness of earthly time I journey,
My fresh footprints illumined by the blessed saints who beckon me:
(include your choicest saints; mine are as follows)
Gentle Aidan and holy Hilda, generous Brigid and kindly Cuthbert,
Holy and wise ones, accompany me.

A voice
The lights fade.
The rumble of creation diminishes.
Mists descend and blanket out what has been.
Heaviness descends.
Your Creator is calling you who leave us,
Is calling you whom we love and release from this world.

The Creator is calling we who remain.
We and you are united in adoration,
Adoration of our Maker and Redeemer.

Mortal friends
God be blessed for the wonder of a life.
God be blessed for all our lives.
May nothing sever our life in You.

One friend
O God in whose arms we die,
Who brought us to birth,
In our grief and shock
Contain, sustain and comfort us,
Embrace us with your love,
Give us hope in our confusion,
And grace to let go into new life.

Mortal friends
The night has passed
And the day lies open before us.

One friend
Let us pray with one heart and voice:

Mortal friends
God of tender consolations,
Take this your dearest soul
That in the company of heaven
He/she may pass from the darkness of mortal death
Into the fullness of everlasting life.

Take your servant from our fretful ways
Into your unending peace.
May he/she now, O God,
Enjoy partnership with you.

Grant him/her your peace past knot of death.
Grant him/her your love unfolding
Pour healing grace upon his/her soul.

Sun of suns, Light of our fleshly being,
Shed light eternal on him/her.

Bathed in your light,
Immersed in your presence,
May he/she know peace of deepest sea,
Peace of Trinity.

Arriving soul to mortal friends
I have died to earth's life.
I am changed.

The perishable is clothed
With the imperishable.
I am changed.

The mortal is clothed
With the immortal.
I am changed.

I have died to your knowledge,
To the mortal and perishable.
From the finite I shall rise
As God wills to Life enduring.
I have died. I am changed.
You too shall die.
You shall be changed.

Lord have mercy.
Christ have mercy.
Lord have mercy.

Mortal friends
Lord have mercy.
Christ have mercy.
Lord have mercy.

Arriving soul
Now my dwelling is with God
And I shall drink from refreshing waters.
Neither pain nor sorrow are my lot,

Neither emptiness nor sighs,
But joy and light unfading.

Arriving soul to mortal friends
May you go forward in your journey on earth:
Father who sought you,
Christ who bought you,
Spirit who taught you,
Hold you in Trinity's heart of love.

Mortal friends
Dear soul, weeping now is done.
Let our song rise with laughter,
Joy and praise to the Creator.
Alleluia. Alleluia. Amen.

PART SIX

* * *

INSPIRING DEATHS

Learn from the dead.

ST COLUMBA

Several religious traditions choose a day each year to celebrate the life of a person whose goodness left a glow after their death. In Christian churches the day chosen for a saint is the day of their death, not of their birth. Their death day is regarded as their birth day, because it marks the birth of their fuller life with God. Here are some stories of people who made glorious exits, or who left a glow after their death.

JESUS (D. 33)

A MEDITATION

No one could die in more physical or emotional pain than Jesus did. What a death! What a human being! Jesus chose to be true to himself, knowing that the cost would be agonizing death by crucifixion.

His seven final sentences have been recorded in the Gospels of the Bible. Many believe that in some way he was representing us, and that he is still with us. He makes himself one with us, even in death. If we make ourselves one with him, even in his dying, our own deaths as well as our lives can be transformed. Thus we use Jesus' dying words as material to help transform our own dying.

1. 'Father, forgive them...' LUKE 23:34
Make a list of people you need to forgive. Look upon all who have hurt you, especially those close to you, with the eyes of Jesus on the cross. See yourself embracing each person with Jesus' love.

2. 'This day you will be with me in paradise' LUKE 23:43
Jesus said this to a criminal who was being crucified beside him and who asked for his help. What is your 'paradise' on earth (your life's work? plans? something you have created?) that you now need to hand over, in order to enter into the 'paradise' God has for you shortly? Empty yourself of it. Ask Jesus to show you what to pray for.

3. 'Mother, behold your son...' JOHN 19:27
Ask Jesus to show you the faces of those who have loved and moulded you. Pick the ones it would be hardest to lose. Say what is on your heart to them. Place their hand in yours, and then in Jesus' hand.

4. 'My God, my God ... Why have you forsaken me?' MATTHEW 27:46
What are you afraid of? Cry it out.

5. 'I thirst' JOHN 19:25
What is your longing? Speak it aloud.

6. 'It is finished' JOHN 19:30

Thank God for the things you have completed in your life. What do you still need to complete? What do you need to hand over to Jesus, asking forgiveness for things left undone or done badly?

7. 'Father, into your hands I commend my spirit' (LUKE 23:46)

Surrender to Father God (who, remember, has a mother's heart) all you need to.

IGNATIUS (D. 107)

Ignatius was the second or third leader of the Christian Church in Antioch, Syria, which was then in the Roman Empire. One day a Roman Emperor decided to get rid of Christian leaders by bringing them to an amphitheatre in Rome where the crowds could watch lions devour them. Can you imagine a more horrible death? Yet Ignatius actually looked forward to death as the start of a much better life.

> The pangs of birth are upon me. Allow me attain the purest light ... for only then will I truly become a human being. Let me imitate the passion of Christ. If any of you have God within you, please understand my longings, and feel for me, for you will know the forces that urge me on.[1]

On his way to Rome, Ignatius wrote to the churches, 'I am in earnest about dying for God – put no obstacles in my way.' He explained that, for him, to die in Jesus Christ was better than all the fame, power or fortune the world could offer.

He prepared for this ordeal by visualizing himself as 'God's wheat, ground fine by the lion's teeth to be made purest bread for Christ'. We may find this hard to understand. So did people in Ignatius' time. That is why he wrote to them that Christians were people who were 'nailed body and soul, as it were, to the cross of the Lord Jesus Christ, rooted and grounded in love by his blood'.

What made this imitating of Christ in death possible was the belief that it was the prelude to resurrection. Ignatius explained:

> [Jesus Christ] was in actual flesh, even after his resurrection. When he appeared to Peter and his companions, he said to them, 'Take hold of me, touch me, and see that I am no bodiless phantom.' And they touched him then and there, and believed, for they had contact with the flesh and blood reality of him. That was how they came by their contempt for death, and proved themselves superior to it.

COLUMBA (D. 597)

Angels prepared Columba for an approaching death. When his many friends learned of this, they sent up unceasing prayers that God would give him longer with them. Columba told them their prayers had been heard and he would be granted another four years on Iona.

Four years later Columba waited until the busy Easter period was over, for he did not want his death to detract from those days. In May he toured the island in a cart, spoke to the workers on the land, and blessed the island. Six days later he visited the barn and thanked God that there was plenty of grain for all his monks. He told his attendant, Diormit, 'This day is called the Sabbath, which means rest. It is indeed a Sabbath for me, for it is the last day of my life. After midnight, when the Lord's Day begins, I shall go the way of our fathers.'[2]

On the way back Columba sat down to rest. His white packhorse came to him and, sensing his master was about to leave this earth, laid his head on Columba's chest and made loud cries of grief. Then Columba ascended the hill and gave a prophetic blessing over the community.

He returned to the monastery and transcribed, as was his custom, some more verses from the Book of Psalms. The last verse he completed was Psalm 34:9, 'They who seek the LORD shall lack no good thing.'

He gave some final words to his brothers, and remained some hours in silence. As soon as the bell tolled for midnight, in a last burst of energy he ran into the unlit church. It was bathed in a heavenly light. He knelt by the altar. Diormit raised Columba's hand and he died blessing his brothers. Their faces were full of grief; Columba's was transfixed with joy.

That night some friends were fishing in the valley of the River Find. They saw an immense pillar of fire, which seemed to illuminate the whole earth like the summer sun at noon. After that the column penetrated the heavens and darkness followed, as if the sun had just set.

MONINNE (D. C.518)

Moninne was one of the earliest saints of Ireland about whom we have reliable information. She was a contemplative linked to a community, and much loved by her own people throughout the region. When they learned that she was on her deathbed, the local rulers and many others gathered round, saying, 'We appeal to you as those who are linked to you by blood and by the spirit, that you will give just one more year of your earthly presence with us. For we know that God will give you whatever you ask. In fact, any of us who has a slave girl will set her free to the Lord, and every man employed as a fighting man will give away a cow in its prime in exchange for your life.'

Moninne gave these good folk the following reply. 'May God bless you for bothering yourselves with my weak self. If you had asked before yesterday, I would have granted your request. But from today I cannot do so. You see, the apostles Peter and Paul have been sent to guide my soul to heaven and they are here with me now. I see them holding a kind of cloth with marvellous gold and artwork. I must go with them to my Lord who sent them.

'God hears your prayers. He will give a life to one of you. I pray God's blessing on your wives, children and homes. I leave you my badgerskin coat and my garden tools. I have no doubt that if you carry these with you when enemies attack, God will deliver you.

'Do not be sad at my leaving you. For I truly believe that Christ, with whom I now go to stay, will give you whatever I ask of Him in heaven no less than when I prayed to Him on earth.'[3]

AIDAN (D. 651)

The early saints of Britain and Ireland offer us an inspired pattern. The Rule of Columba urged each member to prepare for their death. Columba, Cuthbert, Brendan and others were given prophecies about the time and manner of their death. They died triumphantly.

St Aidan, the 'People's Saint', died on 31 August in 651 (the same day that Diana, the 'People's Princess', died in 1997). From his mission base at Lindisfarne he brought Christianity to the pagan English colonizers. He was so greatly loved that, when villagers heard he was on his way, they all ran out to be with him.

Yet Aidan may have died of a stroke, brought on by a broken heart. He died just 11 days after his boss, the fine young Christian king Oswin, was killed by invaders. Aidan was at the Northumbrian royal quarters at Bamburgh, leaning against a cross beam in the church, when he fell ill. To this day the church displays what is said to be that beam. Aidan's friends made a little home in his beloved church at Bamburgh, so he could die there.

Aidan may have felt that his life's work would be wiped out, but, at the moment of Aidan's death, a teenager named Cuthbert saw a vision of angels escorting this holy Christian to heaven. This inspired him to dedicate the rest of his life to Christ's service.

CUTHBERT (D. 687)
AND RAMON (D. 2000)

I visited Brother Ramon, the much-loved friar, on a day when the doctor had brought bad news. He knew he was going to die, even though he had received laying on of hands for healing.

'You see, Ray,' he told me, 'I *did* receive a healing – the warmth went right through my body. But then the Lord said to me, "Who do you think you are to assume you can have a complete healing like Naaman, in the Bible? I give you a sacramental healing, I give you my touch every day, but you are not going to get completely healed. So there!" So you see, Ray, I have a great adventure ahead of me.'

Then he asked me to send him something I had not expected – a photograph of the island where Cuthbert spent the last years of his life. I made two guesses as to why he asked for that photograph. I guessed that he hankered to be back in the borderlands, as he had once been as a hermit, where land meets sea. I also wondered whether he wished to retrace the last months of Cuthbert's life on Farne Island, so faithfully recorded by a monk of Lindisfarne.

Like Ramon, Cuthbert, in obedience to the Church, left his hermitage by the sea. For two brief years as bishop, Cuthbert brought faith, healing and love to multitudes and greatly developed the mission begun by Aidan.

Three months before his death, his intuition told him he must resign and live alone again in the solitude of Farne Island. There he prepared for death. He suffered a painful illness. For the best part of a week his only food was a few onions. His Lindisfarne friends, at first prevented by storms from reaching him, eventually arrived by boat to be with him for his last days.

Cuthbert told them it was necessary that he had been on his own, for he had fought against demons more terrible than any he had known in his life. He had fought them, and he had overcome them. His parting words were, 'Always keep God's peace and love among you ... send guests on their way with kindness and friendship ... Never think you are superior to others.'[4]

God bless our hermits Cuthbert and Ramon.

HILDA (D. 680)

Hilda, whose life as Abbess of Whitby brought radiance to the whole of Britain, was afflicted with debilitating fever for six years before she died. Yet every day she gave thanks to God in public and private. On her last day she received Holy Communion, exhorted her sisters, and went joyfully to her Lord.

Thirteen miles away, a nun was woken up from sleep by the sound of a bell which was tolled when someone had died. She saw a vision of light streaming down from heaven into a monastery whose roof had been removed. In the midst of this light was the soul of Hilda, escorted by angels. The nun roused her sisters, who spent the rest of the night in prayer and praise for Hilda. At dawn some brothers arrived to announce Hilda's death. The historian Bede comments,

By a beautiful conjunction of events God arranged it that while some witnessed Hilda's departure from this life, others witnessed her entry into the everlasting life of the spirit.[5]

CAEDMON (D. 680)

Hilda had helped a farm labourer named Caedmon, who could not read or write, to become the first pop singer in the English language. His Bible songs captivated many gatherings. His life, too, came to a beautiful end that same year.

Caedmon surprised his friends when he asked to go into the monastery hospice, for he was still chirpy and on his feet. But God had shown Caedmon that he had not long left to live.

On Caedmon's first day in the hospice, he joked with every resident and carer until midnight. Then he asked if they had the sacrament of Holy Communion in the house. 'Why now?' the helpers replied. 'You are not going to die yet, you seem to be in good health and spirits.'

But Caedmon took the 'bread of eternal life' in his hand, and he asked if everyone's heart was at peace with his and quite free from anger. He told them, 'My heart is at peace, little children, with all God's servants.'

Caedmon asked how long it would be before the brothers began to sing their night praises, and was told it would not be long. 'Good,' he said. 'Then let us wait for that hour.'

He signed himself with the cross, lay his head on his pillow, slept for a while, and ended his life in the gentle silence.

A BOY (D. C.690)

There is a growing fear that fast-track gene manipulation could lead to fatal epidemics. We need to remind ourselves that our lands have been swept by epidemics in the past.

A fatal plague swept through the Sussex area of Britain in the seventh century. It decimated the members of a monastery at Selsey. As a result, at the beginning of August that year, the remaining monks decided to pray to God for three days without even taking food.

While they were praying, a little boy who had recently become a Christian and who was dying of the plague saw two loving, radiant people come to him. They said their names were Peter and Paul. 'Don't fear death,' they told him, 'for we have come to take you to heaven today. But first take Holy Communion so that you will be given strength to support you on your journey.'

Peter and Paul, those two apostles of Christ, asked the boy to tell the monks that their prayers had been answered. None of them would die of the plague, only himself. They explained that his journey to heaven and the monks' recovery was a divine favour, brought about not only through their prayers, but also through the prayers of a holy king of their people, St Oswald. For it was on that very day, 6 August, that Oswald had been killed in battle against tyrants and had been taken to the joys of heaven. The divine visitors suggested that in future the monastery should celebrate this answer to their prayers and the 'heavenly birthday' of Oswald on 6 August.

The boy told all this to the Prior. He looked up various records, and found that the Northumbrians' King Oswald had indeed died on that day. With great joy, the monks made celebration, and on every 6 August after that they held special services of Holy Communion to keep alive the memory of Oswald.

BEDE (D. 735)

The great historian Bede was dying. He was a monk at the Jarrow monastery. He suffered frequent attacks of breathlessness, but continued to be cheerful and to give thanks to God night and day. When he woke up he would spread out his hands in prayer and repeat verses from the Bible. He used to sing, 'O King of glory, Lord of might, who ascended in triumph to heaven, leave us not without comfort, but send us the Spirit of truth. Alleluia!' And he often repeated these words: 'The Lord disciplines those he loves,' and, 'I am not afraid to die, for the God we serve is good.'

There were two books he was translating from Latin into English: *The Gospel of John* and an anthology of Bishop Isidore's book *The Wonders of Nature*. He was keen to finish these, because he did not want his spiritual children to miss out on them after he was gone.

On the Tuesday before Ascension Day he became much worse, but carried on dictating as usual. At daybreak on the Wednesday he gave instructions that the writing and transcribing be finished without delay. The scribes worked at this until 9 p.m. Then one of his assistants said to him, 'There is still one chapter to be completed, but I guess it would be too hard for you to go through this now.'

'It is not hard,' Bede replied. 'Take your pen and write fast.'

At 3 a.m. he shared out his little trinkets with various brothers and told them that it was time for him to depart, for he longed to see Christ his King in all his beauty.

Then his assistant, Wilbert, said to him, 'There is still one sentence that we have not written down.'

Bede said, 'Write it.'

After a while, Wilbert said, 'There. Now it is written.'

'Good, it is finished,' Bede replied. 'You have spoken the truth. Hold my head in your hands, for it is a delight to sit in the place where I have prayed so often.'

And so, upon the floor of his cell, singing 'Glory to the Father and to the Son and to the Holy Spirit', he breathed his last.[6]

MUM (D. 1971)

Our Mum lived alone in a village not far from Bognor Regis, in Sussex. She looked young and had barely turned 60. Our Father had died two years earlier. Her three children were in far-flung places and I, in London, was the nearest. We knew she had cancer, but the doctor assured her that a routine operation would be successful. I planned to visit her on my next day off as she convalesced. For some inexplicable reason, however, her blood pressure dived during the operation, and she died on the operating table. There had to be an inquest.

My boss returned from holiday early so that I could go to her home at once; there would be so much to sort out. Stunned and numbed, I arrived at her house. To my astonishment, I found that it had been completely cleared: there was virtually nothing for me to sort out or throw away. Moreover, the black metal box which contained her papers and her will was placed, waiting for me, at the top of the stairs.

By some intuition or divine intimation, she had been prepared for her sudden departure from this earth. She was so smiling, peaceful and unselfish. She thought of us more than of herself before she went to that operation.

I wish I had been able to say goodbye, but she knew that I loved her dearly. While we moved out her things, held the funeral, put the house up for sale, and still, long afterwards, her sweetness stays with us.

COLIN

Colin MacCallum worked briefly as a lawyer and then as a doctor. His mind was clouded by the necessity for logic and what he called 'facts'. God was only a possibility, so there was a void in his life. This void was hidden because he was a human dynamo and never stood still for a minute. Work, academic study, renovating the house and being a father crammed his life.

Until, that is, illness gave him time to think. As a result of this thinking, he gave his life to God. The change in him was unbelievable. Over a period of 10 days, he went through a deep spiritual preparation for death. He had no fear in dying; he trusted God completely.

Those who visited Colin expected a broken, dispirited man. Instead they found a warmth and inspiration that had never been there before. His body weak and dying, and depending completely on others, Colin proved at his weakest to be more powerful than ever before in his life. That strength came from outside himself. It came from God.

His parish priest, Stuart Burns, anointed Colin and laid hands on his abdomen. Stuart's hands shook violently, inexplicably, and he was unable to remove them for several minutes. Was this a sign of God's power being made perfect in weakness?

The most marvellous experience of all occurred just before Colin died. The consultant informed his wife Marilyn that, owing to the high doses of drugs, he thought Colin would not now regain consciousness. Colin, however, suddenly and completely came out of unconsciousness and spoke rationally and clearly. His face was radiant, healthy and shining strangely white, his eyes wide open and filled with indescribable joy. Was it a vision of God? He struggled to tell what he could see – but his face and eyes told more than his words.

To his wife and his priest he spoke clearly: 'I am going now. It's marvellous, marvellous. It's marvellous!' His joy was so infectious that they could only laugh with him. Marilyn felt urgently that she should not hold him back, but should send him on his way in that moment.

This story is based on notes written and circulated by Marilyn. They conclude as follows:

How could he die so happily when he had so much to live for? He had an insight into Eternity with God. He was filled with, powered by and totally subject to the love of God.

If you knew Colin as a doctor or a friend, don't let his dying count for nothing. While looking forward to death he longed for just one hour of normal living to visit his patients and friends – to plead with them to stop and think. He felt that some, including himself, had got life all wrong. He had realized in his suffering and dying that if the love of God were made the focal point of people's lives, they would be *living well*.

A DANCER (D. PRE-1994)

A care worker in a Paris hospice for the terminally ill says she sees miracles every day. One of these 'miracles' was a man named Jean. Jean had been a dancer. Now at death's door, he was in acute pain and had horrible, putrefying lesions all over his legs and lower body. Yet he had extraordinary moral strength. He made enormous efforts to get to the meal table, where he told stories. He used to say, 'Come on, guys, our bodies have gone to hell, but our spirits are free.' He was full of *joie de vivre*.

Just before he died he called a friend and asked him to hold his hands and dance with him. He wanted to remain a dancer to the very end. Jean lifted himself a little and, with his friend's help, began with all his heart to make his arms dance.

His friend wept. 'Dance, dance,' Jean kept saying as their linked arms swayed from left to right. Then Jean smiled a magnificent, transcendent smile, collapsed on his pillow, and died.[7]

> They cut me down but I leap up high –
> I am the life that'll never, never die.
> I'll live in you if you'll live in me,
> I am the Lord of the Dance, said he.
>
> Dance then wherever you may be,
> I am the Lord of the Dance, said he,
> And I'll lead you all, wherever you may be
> And I'll lead you all in the dance, said he.
> SYDNEY CARTER[8]

NORMA (D. 1991)

Many people have heard of Noel Proctor, the uneducated Irishman who became a famous British prison chaplain, for which he received the MBE. Many hundreds of prisoners found a faith through Noel, and loved him. When the riots which began in the chapel and destroyed Strangeways Prison occurred, Noel was devastated and turned to his wife for support.

What fewer people know is that Noel's wife Norma has a moving story to tell, also. At the time of the Strangeways riots she knew she had cancer, but at first she kept this from Noel in order to support him in his own need.

Norma kept a diary of the last years of her life. Here are some extracts from it – written, of course, before the latest improvements in cancer treatment.

1 April 1990, Strangeways riot

I have known for some months now that I have a secondary spread of the cancer. I knew when Noel went to Withington Hospital to have a Rodent ulcer removed from his face. I couldn't tell him how I was when he needed me, and with God's help I would be there with him.

The family came first, although watching the changes in my body I know there is no recession of the cancer. My strength and my peace I find daily in the assurance of Christ's love for me and my faith in him is steadfast. 'So far thy hand has led me, sure it will still lead me on.'

Various days in September 1990

Please God let me live until December for Helen's graduation.

I have had a dry irritating cough for some weeks now and I am breathless when I climb stairs or go up an incline. I know my condition is worsening and I want to keep it hidden from my family for just a little longer. When Helen finishes her teaching practice, then I will tell them how ill I am...

Noel and I have had a few days' holiday in County Durham visiting old haunts and old friends. My cough has been particularly troublesome and I know I haven't looked well. Noel, I so want to tell you I am ill but you have been through so much, how can I heap more sorrow on you?

Noel said, 'Norma, is this cough worrying you?' and I told him as gently as I could of the secondary spread. I was amazed as he looked at me and said, 'Yes, I know. I just wondered when you would tell me.' I explained to Noel that the only treatment on offer to me was chemotherapy, and I know about cytotoxic [anti-cancer] drugs and their awful side effects. I have always said I would refuse this treatment as I want quality in my life, not quantity.

We loved and cuddled each other and we wept together and committed it to the Lord. Noel knows I'm no quitter. I shall fight in God's strength for a while longer. When the time is right we shall tell the girls.

I try not to think that I am dying with cancer; rather that I am living with cancer. God's grace is available to me each day and I'm taking it one day at a time.

As I look back on my life, I have had so much, loving parents, grandparents, family relatives, a good marriage, a loving and devoted husband, three beautiful and talented daughters. I have been totally fulfilled.

What is faith if it is not reaching out into the darkness of doubt and despair crying, 'Lord I don't understand, but hold onto me for I trust you Lord.'

I have asked for a healing service in our home on the Wednesday and asked to be anointed with oil (according to the Scriptures). Noel asked that he be anointed with oil also. Wednesday came and my closest friends Annie, Alan and Flo, Stephen, Noel and I met in our lounge. God's peace was already filling my heart and mind. We had a time of praise and worship then three readings from Scripture; a time of confession and waiting upon God, then they each in turn anointed Noel and me with oil and the sign of the cross was made on our foreheads.

Noel, bless him, so warm and loving, keeps his thoughts and feelings hidden. He is so grateful to God for each day we have. 'Lord in my anxiety, I plead spare my life for a little longer. Please don't crush Noel.' Then I realize I see things with only limited sight. I see only my situation. I need to pray for wider vision knowing God sees the whole panorama of our life. He is the Alpha and the Omega. 'Lord I surrender to you. You are in control of my situation. Thank you, Lord.'

Someone has said that 'Faith is trusting when we can't understand.' At times it's almost impossible. 'Oh God help me to hold on to you!!'

It's good to reach out in the night and hear words of comfort and reassurance; to feel Noel take hold of my hand and squeeze it just to let me know he cares.

Lord, minister to Noel, impart your strength and grace to him. He gives himself unsparingly to all. Anoint us both in your Holy Spirit. Jesus, I'm tired, but I rest in You. Thank you for your peace.

I feel so weak, I wish my appetite would improve. It seems strange to me, for however poorly I have been in the past I could always eat. I don't want to burden my family and friends. I long for healing, to be stronger and even if I don't ask why with my lips, my heart is continually questioning. I think of the words of that beautiful hymn:

O Love that will not let me go
I rest my weary soul on Thee
I give Thee back the life I owe
That in Thine ocean depths its flow
May richer, fuller be.

O Joy that seekest me through pain
I dare not ask to fly from Thee
I trace the rainbow through the rain
And feel the promise is not vain
That morn shall tearless be.

O Lord I don't pretend to understand and I hate how I feel, so in this darkness Lord I reach out my hand to you, just hold me tight. I love you, Jesus, but I don't understand your dealings with me.

As usual I voiced what I felt before my God (I never see the need for pretence before Him, for his Word tells me He knows what I am thinking) and in my frustration I cried, 'Lord if this is living, please let me die, I don't want to feel perpetually weary.

I want to live.' On the Wednesday of the meeting I felt really good. Emotional, but at peace. We sang before we parted, 'In the Name of Jesus we have the victory'.

...This morning I am off duty and from my bedroom I hear the happy noise of children on their way to school. I have been talking with the Lord and listening to Him. I was reading Psalm 34 in the night, verses 8–9 are beautiful with the promises of God. I have asked Him to touch my cancerous body. I so long to be healed, to awaken to vitality.

I don't need a façade with the Lord. He sees right into my heart. He doesn't see me as a wife and mother, or as a ward sister. He sees me as His weak and vulnerable child and He cuddles me in His love. Lord, I need your strength, just hold me and let me know you are with me always.

18 December 1990

Helen graduated at Leeds University. I felt so ill that day but nothing was stopping me going to the proud event. Helen looked lovely. So young, so full of life. I was a proud mother and so thankful to God that I had been spared to see this day.

January 1991

I began to feel poorly again and noticed my abdomen was swollen. I was taken into Christie's again and 1.5 gallons of fluid was aspirated from my tummy. I felt so weak, I couldn't stand and became very despondent. I was inundated with cards and flowers and the assurance of hundreds praying for me. Yet in the darkness I cried out, 'Lord have you forgotten me?' and immediately His words came, 'A mother may forget the child she bears but I will never forget you. I have carved you on the palms of my hands.'

April 1991

Time has passed and now it is April. Many visits to Christie Hospital to have fluid drained from my lungs and abdomen. Dr Stewart is always helpful and honest – he pulls no punches and raises no false hopes.

The initial weeks were dreadful, the treatment made me so ill. I lost three stone and looked awful.

I have good days and bad ones. I know hundreds are still praying for my healing and I am comforted. When I came home from my last stay at Christie's, the dining room had been made into a bedroom for me. No more climbing stairs. It's a haven and I feel God's presence with me at all times.

Noel had wept so often seeing my weakness and then one night he told the Lord, 'I hand Norma over to you Lord. No more pleading and struggling. You are in control of our situation and I leave her with you.' He told me of an indescribable peace filling his heart and the very presence of God filling his room.

I awakened the other night to hear the words of St Paul echoing in my bedroom. 'I have fought a good fight. I have finished the course. I have kept the faith, henceforth there is laid up for me a crown of righteousness which the Lord the righteous judge will give me and not to me only but to all who love His appearing.'

I know I am dying, as my family knows it too, but I am in His hands. I am not struggling, only resting in Him.

I have lived a fulfilled life, as a woman, a nurse, a wife, a mother, above all as a follower of Jesus Christ since I was 13 years old.

None has been more loved, no one has been made to feel so complete.

Noel Proctor is the only man I have ever loved and I could not begin to describe his devotion to me. Noel is and has been God's precious gift to me. Our relationship has the stamp of God's approval all over it.

This is what I pray my girls will find, fulfilment in life and completeness in their Saviour.

Noel continues the diary.

We had a long talk one evening after our prayers about the subject of death. Norma has no fear of it, only of the process of dying, and all its indignities.

It was Saturday evening and with Norma in bed in the dining room surrounded by her family photos and her antiques gathered over the years, we had our own prayer time together, when suddenly she said, 'I haven't heard you singing round the house lately.' My reply was that there hasn't been much to sing about, when she said, 'Sing "Great is Thy faithfulness".' I did try but after a couple of lines I broke down in tears. Suddenly her weak voice took over and encouraged me to sing on. Helen came in and played the piano. It was nearly 11.30 p.m. when we finished praising and worshipping the Lord Jesus. As I climbed the stairs I could not help but admire her strength and faith.

I shared this with the lads in the prison at the Sunday service, and the reactions were remarkable. Jimmy asked to see me and told me of his endeavour to pray earlier in the week, and how he had opened his Good News Bible seeking for help and comfort. It opened at Isaiah 43 and verse 2 stood out to him – 'When you pass through the waters I will be with you...' After talking of both our experiences, he and I prayed together and he surrendered his life to Jesus. So it does show the spin-off from our musical session!

Monday night was difficult. At one point when we came to Norma she was saying, 'I want my Mummy.' I got really worried but Sue reassured me that this often happens when people are seriously ill.

Norma was taken to a hospice, and later Noel was called for. He continues:

I sat at the bedside and read aloud to Norma her favourite Romans Chapter 8, sobbing as I moved from promise to promise in that wonderful passage.

I looked at Norma and perhaps it was the light or the fact that I had just kissed her on the lips, but she appeared to be smiling – she was in the Presence of the Lord Jesus whom she loved so much.

NIGEL (D. 1993)

Nigel left his parents' village home and set up his own flat in our neighbourhood on the advice of a counsellor. He needed to live his own life, and to work through his personal problems, in the framework of a cosmopolitan but friendly community.

Nigel loved life – jazz, football, a wild life. He was a songwriter, singer and guitarist. He had immaturities, but also some wonderful qualities. Unknown to anyone, however, inoperable bone cancer was already eating away at his body when he came among us.

Nobody suspected that his 'back pains' were more than they seemed. Very late in the day, his true condition was diagnosed. Suddenly, one Saturday morning, he told me, 'I'm trying to come to terms with being terminal.'

FUNNIES

I gave Nigel *carte blanche* to make my computer his own for the last weeks of his life. He started a file headed 'Funnies'. This began:

> **Following being advised by the doctor of the seriousness of my illness I phoned my friend Sue to tell her the news. One of her first remarks was, 'My friend Anita is a lawyer, she could do a will for you. She also needs the money.'**

Nigel thought this was amusing, but it also reflects the fact that he was not in denial, and neither was his friend Sue.

ILLNESS PROGRESSION

On another computer file Nigel documented the progression of his illness. The first entry was April 1992:

> **Bad neck pain following long drive with friends.**

Then came other entries:

June
Painkillers were prescribed.

December
Stopped work.

New Year's Eve
In too much pain to go out. Spent evening alone, drinking. Also took eight paracetamol. Damage minimized because dose was spread around the *Monty Python and the Holy Grail* film. More of a cry for help rather than a suicide attempt.

January 93
Collapsed in pain one evening. Called out doctor. Friend (Bill) waited with me for doctor. Injected with pethodine to knock me out for the night and ordered to lie on the floor for 48 hours. Phoned another friend (John) who suggested I stayed with his family. Bill drove me over. Stayed almost three weeks.

February 93
Depressed, attempted to return to own house. Heating broken and I'm too weak to fix it. Took eight diazapam and eight codydramol. Moved on to Church House to stay with one of my ministers.

One and a half weeks after scan, received a call from doctor at 8:30 a.m. – can I see him immediately. Results indicate illness similar to Hodgkin's disease and bones look 'a bit moth-eaten'. Appointment made with Dr Ostrowski (cancer specialist) at Norfolk and Norwich hospital for the following Tuesday.

Sunday 14 February
Went to Red Lion pub in Thorpe with John C. and Sue to see the Vintage Hot Orchestra, which was my custom before I became too ill. Met Beryl and her friend Ken Gibbs at pub. Band leader Ian Bell gave me a copy of their latest recording.

16 February
Saw Dr Ostrowski. He told me that I am 'one of life's mysteries'. They are treating my illness as some form of bone cancer but stressed that it was unproven. I was shown bone scan pictures and

told that the black areas were 'hot spots', i.e. problem sites. I was shocked when he switched on the light-box to illuminate the pictures. Only the arms, legs and skull were completely clear. Commenced radiotherapy.

19 February

First ever operation. Removal of lymph node from neck for biopsy. Touch and go regarding use of general or local anaesthetic, decided I was a big boy and opted for a local. Experienced amazing array of emotions during op., ranging from extreme fear to joy. Following the op., I asked the surgeon (Stephen Mitchell) if it was a girl.

8 March

Saw Dr Ostrowski ... He offered two options of treatment: firstly, to do nothing and see how it develops; and secondly to administer chemotherapy. He felt that the best thing to do was nothing...

16 March

I've been talking to a friend who has suffered from Muscular Dystrophy all his life (he's now 45). He says that one of the hardest parts of long-term illness is adjusting to new steps of deterioration as they come along. The return of the lump last night for me marks one such step. It is the coming to terms with the fact that some of my treatment has been beaten by the cancer. This does not mean to say that further treatment will not be more effective. I now know I'm in a battle which I cannot ignore and also one in which I've suffered a defeat. I went to bed with death written in hand-writing and I woke up with it written in capitals.

I had a visit from my doctor just after lunch and now I feel the tiniest amount of hope. Underneath it all, in fact, I think I'm desperate for hope, so maybe I really haven't come to terms with the idea of death after all.

18 March

Saw Dr Agnew at the Priscilla Bacon Hospice. She was able to put me a bit more in the picture regarding my illness. I have cancer in my bones although the site of the primary is likely to be elsewhere … She advised me of the emotional states I could expect to go through especially as I'm relatively young (31). Firstly shock/disbelief; then anger; then depression; and finally a general acceptance. I mentioned to her that in a rather morbid way, I've found a new identity in the illness and part of me is actually enjoying being ill. She said that this is quite normal because there are advantages to this, like an increase in attention and a freedom to do what I like 'because I am ill'. She also advised me to expect a tailing off of other people's interest as they notice little change in me because it's a long-term problem and not something short like a cold. Made another appointment to see her on 8 April, 2 p.m.

FINAL DETAILS

Nigel created a third file on the computer headed 'Final Details', which began:

> This may seem a bit grim but I feel it right to note down a few things which are important to me that will be outside the scope of a will.
>   This does not mean I've given up hope on getting well; I'm just taking advantage of the opportunity while it's available to me. I can't sign a computer to confirm that I'm Nigel Roper so you'll just have to trust that what follows agrees with what you know of me.

Then Nigel stated where he wished his funeral to take place, which charity the collection money should be sent to, and his ideas about songs for the funeral. This section began:

> I have to confess that I'm not a great fan of most of the Christian songs sung around the churches, however there are one or two that are quite special to me…

He made a list of people he would like to be contacted if or when he died, and a list of his financial details. Like many people, it dawned on him that 'I'm worth much more in death than in life.'

In a fourth file Nigel noted down phrases that spoke to him from books he was reading.

Not Once but Twice by Derek Williams recounted how Derek twice recovered from serious cancer. Nigel noted these sentences:

> The chemotherapy had rendered him sterile. *(To be rendered sterile was not something Nigel took to easily.)*

> Hushing up is unhealthy.

> Where there's hope, fight. In my situation you fight like mad; there's something unnatural about being cut down in the prime of life.

> God has transformed it (death) into a gateway to his presence.

From *An Evil Cradling* by Brian Keenan, the Belfast journalist who was taken hostage in Lebanon, Nigel noted:

> In the face of death but not because of it they (men) explode with passionate life, conquering despair with insane humour.

From Selwyn Hughes' Bible Notes *Every Day with Jesus* for 3 March 1993:

> ...we must hold fast to the things that are fixed. The cross is a fixed point; an anchor sunk in solid bedrock.

From a book entitled *Writing to Inspire*:

> Dare to dream so big that only God's Holy Spirit can accomplish that goal through your writing.

'FAITH ON THE SLAB'

As death approached, a desire to be a writer was born. Yet all that seemed to await Nigel was an operation. This gave him a flicker of hope that he might live, but I think deep down he knew it was unlikely. Nigel turned that operation into the first (and only) chapter of a book. He chose as his title 'Faith on the Slab'.

Faith on the slab. It brings to mind the image of a great man of faith holding on courageously to his Lord in the face of horrendous suffering. With his breastplate of righteousness firmly in place, his shield of faith paraded before him and his loins thoroughly girded up, he marches off to face the foe ... Hallelujah!

Unfortunately the real scenario is slightly different. The fearless warrior happens to be me, and I've never been so scared in my life. I'm flat out on the operating table waiting to have something removed from my neck. No ... not my Norwich City Football Club scarf, it's a lymph node which has decided to claim its inheritance early and depart for sunnier climes. My loins are ungirded as never before, mainly because of the ill-fitting hospital gown. The surgeon whispers menacingly the phrase that patients everywhere have come to dread: 'Would you turn your head to the left please?' and there before me it stands, poised for combat and laden with its glittering armoury ... the instrument trolley!

As the operation commences my fear begins to rise. The work seems to be taking an eternity and I'm starting to panic. Even the most well meaning of friends cannot be with me here, and however comforting and jolly the theatre staff may be, I'm still alone. Then suddenly God takes his heavenly syringe and injects into the very heart of my fearfulness a reminder of his constant faithfulness: 'I'm still here.' These words awaken in me a level of faith in Jesus that would have been undiscoverable outside of this experience. All I can do is praise him, for I have been brought to the realization that my faith is a real one – even on the slab.

Brian Keenan in his book *An Evil Cradling* refers to the creation of his work as being part of his own healing. I have also found this to be the case. The categorization of the various black, white and grey aspects of my life especially at this time of sickness has proved to be a very therapeutic untangling of my inner self.

I find it hard to keep pace with God as he continues to unveil deep truths relevant to seemingly every area of my existence. As I write, the current diagnosis is that I have some form of malignant cancer, but because it has yet to be identified exactly, the view of the specialist is to do nothing and see how it develops. In some respects living with this uncertainty is harder than being told that I have a set period before I die. I am forced to live one day at a time. Facing the future is like walking along a mist-shrouded cliff-top: the next step could take me over the edge and into eternity. Any plans I may have must be set free to be blown along like a hot-air balloon and brought to earth at a location of the Holy Spirit's choosing.

This is one of the great gifts of Christian living: we are saved from an uncertain future because God promises to take care of our every need. When death suddenly parades itself on the stage of life, I am compelled to take notice and either to live out God's word or to worry myself into an even earlier grave. In John 10:10 Jesus says that he has come in order that *everyone* might have abundant life. This does not exclude cancer victims. If we decide to ignore what's on offer then we create our own abundant hell.

As I mentioned earlier, the illness is changing my perspective of many things around me. I hope to share some of these discoveries, together with a little background information to my life, in the following chapters.

There were no following chapters. Death came quickly. Yet that blessed computer, and conversations which people remembered, give us a glimpse of an emerging heavenly career. Another folder of Nigel's headed 'Thoughts' contained the following:

WHY?!!!! I'm tired. I ache. I feel old. I've had enough.
I want to walk over that bridge into eternal peace.

Ever since I was told of the seriousness of my condition I've always felt that I wouldn't recover. This presented me with a problem when good, reliable, sound Christian friends tell me that when they pray for me they feel very positive with regard to my healing. This evening I had a conversation with Ray which has helped to marry these seemingly differing viewpoints together. This life is a preparation for the next. The way in which I allow God to use me here will have a direct bearing on the way I'm to be used in the next life. In fact, rather than drawing a line between the two lives, they can be seen as two parts of one eternal existence; death is merely the doorway from one phase into the other. Thanks to Jesus the unseen second phase need hold no fear for us; unless we choose to ignore his sacrifice. In the light of this, the term 'healing' takes on an eternal nature and has more to do with the refining of the whole life in preparation for the next phase than mere physical healing for the present time. I do not dismiss the possibility of physical healing although my gut-feeling is that it won't happen. Of course, the time scale of events is an unknown factor to me. I am learning to live one day at a time and to be thankful for what each day brings.

There also appears to be an acceleration in the way God is dealing with problems in my life, as well as giving me new revelations. By this I mean that I'm aware of an almost constant stream of input from him – it's as though time is short.

However, I do not feel that all this constitutes a negative attitude on my part; on the contrary, I find it hard to think of anything more positive than to be able to embrace death – the ultimate evil – with joy. Not a kind of suicidal joy but something more akin to what Paul says in Philippians 1:23: 'I desire to be with Christ, which is better by far...'

Death becomes like the day the exam results come through the post and you see how well you've done, the difference being that because of Jesus there is no need to fail. Then you go on to your eternal career: a career more magnificent than anyone can imagine – it has to be: it's got to last for ever.[9]

THE 'SWEET PEA' (D. 1999)

> God uses the briefest ... life as powerfully and significantly as He
> uses a whole long life of work and achievement.
> ARCHBISHOP MICHAEL RAMSEY

We can prepare for our own death, not only by imagining our own
deathbed, but also by writing letters to those who have died. As you
read the following stories about 'The Sweet Pea', ask yourself what
lessons you can learn for your own death and for those who will
mourn for you.

Mandy and Glynn had for years longed to have a baby and asked
their friends to pray for this. At last, beautiful little Eleanor was
born. But she was brain damaged and only survived for two weeks.

How does one react to such tragedy? Often parents in this situation rage at everyone and at God. Those around Mandy and Glynn
could not understand their behaviour. For, although they were
heartbroken, and Glynn did experience anger, they let their pain
become a way of sharing the hurts of others. By keeping their hearts
open, they felt carried along by others and by God. Something
beautiful grew out of something ugly.

Throughout those two weeks they held Eleanor, talked and
prayed with her, photographed and played music to her. When she
died, the staff invited Mandy to wash her, and nurses who had no
task to perform came to Eleanor's room because they sensed a special
presence there.

Mandy and Glynn arranged a Service of Thanksgiving for
Eleanor at their local church, St Paul's at the Crossing, Walsall. Over
150 friends came, and they received over 400 cards.

People asked, 'How can you give thanks for such an untimely
death?' They were not giving thanks for her death, they said, but for
her life. Even in those nine months in the womb and two weeks out
of it, there were signs and wonders.

For example, the service began with a recording of 'The Trumpet
Shall Sound' from Handel's *Messiah*. Why? Because, when Eleanor
heard this piece at Christmas, she jumped for joy in her mother's
womb. The words to this music are:

The trumpet shall sound
and the dead shall be raised incorruptible;
and we shall be changed.
For this corruptible must put on incorruption,
and this mortal must put on immortality.

FROM I CORINTHIANS 15:52–3

THE CHILD GOD LOANED

Somebody sent Mandy the following poem, which was read at the
Thanksgiving Service for Eleanor.

'I'll lend you for a little while a child of mine,' God said,
'for you to love, the while she lives,
and mourn for when she's dead.
It may be two or three weeks, or forty-two or three,
but will you, till I call her back, take care of her for me?
She'll bring her charms to gladden you,
and should her stay be brief,
you'll always have her memories, as a solace in your grief.
I cannot promise she will stay, since all from earth return,
but there are lessons taught below I want this child to learn.
I've looked this whole world over
in my search for teachers true
and from the crowds along the way, I have chosen you.
Now will you give her all your love
and not think the labour vain
nor hate me when I come to take this lent child back again?'

I fancy that I heard them say, 'Dear God, thy will be done.
For all the joys this child will bring, the risk of grief we'll run.
We will shelter her with tenderness,
we'll love her while we may,
and for all the happiness we've ever known
we'll ever grateful stay.
But should her Maker call her much sooner than we'd planned
we will brave the bitter grief that comes and try to understand.'

ANONYMOUS

Mandy and Glynn wrote letters to their beloved daughter. These they themselves read out at the Thanksgiving Service.

Glynn's letter included these words:

> My darling, darling daughter Eleanor, so much to say, so much to remember in two short weeks. You were such a wanted child...
>
> That very first night after your birth my life changed, you had captured my heart in a way I never thought possible...
>
> You amazed the doctors with your fight for life. I was proud to be your personal trainer. It was a great thrill to feel your strength growing as we exercised every six hours...
>
> It seems to me it was your mission to open people up to love ... I had never known such a depth of love until you were born my precious little one, and I know that you have changed my world and the way I look at things for ever.
>
> When we went to register your birth we were so overcome with pride as they filled in the columns with us as father and mother. That is something that cannot be taken from us and we will treasure for ever.
>
> Darling Ellie, there are so many things I want to say but my heart would break ... God bless you my beloved daughter, you carry my heart with you.

Mandy's letter to Eleanor included these words:

> I so enjoyed having you inside me, I was so proud to be pregnant. Each morning when I bathed I would talk to you, even sing to you...
>
> Let me tell you about your Dad. He is the kindest man I have ever met in all my life. He is caring, considerate, gentle, selfless and a man of great faith...
>
> You have been given a task to carry out that no one could have guessed ... You have brought people together ... You healed wounds that we longed to be closed...
>
> The most beautiful and painful moment of my life came when your Dad and I held you in our arms that last hour and a half. You were so very beautiful my little one. Your Dad and I prayed

and sang to you ... Your Dad prayed for you not to be afraid but to walk to Jesus ... We like to think of you with your tambourine, dancing and singing before the Lord.

* * *

Mandy and Glyn wrote to their deceased baby.

Are there things locked in your own heart which you were never able to say to a loved one who passed on? It is not too late to write a letter even now. Here is some space to do so.

My letter to...

Signed...

PLANTING SEEDS IN MEMORY

The gardener asked, 'Who plucked this flower?'
The Master said, 'I plucked it for myself,'
and the gardener held his peace.
ANONYMOUS

During Eleanor's brief life, Mandy sometimes called her 'Sweet Pea' because she was fragile but sweet and lovely. This led to an inspiration which gave their many friends, who did not know how to put their feelings into words, a way to remember Eleanor thankfully. Mandy and Glynn gave everyone sweet pea seeds in a packet labelled, 'Please grow these sweet peas in your garden in memory of Eleanor...'

We planted our packet in our garden at The Open Gate, on the Holy Island of Lindisfarne. All who planted these had time to savour the wonder of that little life in a way that surely rejoiced the Creator's heart.

Why not grow something beautiful in memory of a loved one?

Why not suggest a flower you would one day like a loved one to plant in memory of you?

The seed I would like others to plant in memory of me is:

By taking pains to savour the wonder of even a fleeting little life, we learn not to hurry through our own life and its departing, but to give it, too, the value it is due.

EPILOGUE

I believe that at the deepest level of our being we can choose life or death.

God bless you, and give us each our own good death.

Remember that with God, death is a comma, not a full stop.

I hope that this book will encourage you to live fully and to die well.

If you would like to know what other resources we have here on this Holy Island of saints and resurrections, please contact us.

Ray Simpson,
The Community of Aidan and Hilda,
The Open Gate,
Holy Island,
Berwick-upon-Tweed TD15 2SD

A BLESSING FOR DEATH

I pray that you will have the blessing of being consoled and sure about your own death.

May you know in your soul that there is no need to be afraid.

When your time comes, may you be given every blessing and shelter that you need.

May there be a beautiful welcome for you in the home that you are going to. You are not going somewhere strange. You are going back to the home that you never left.

May you have a wonderful urgency to live your life to the full. May you live compassionately and creatively and transfigure everything that is negative within you and about you.

When you come to die may it be after a long life.

May you be peaceful and happy and in the presence of those who really care for you.

May your going be sheltered and your welcome assured.

May your soul smile in the embrace of your *anam cara*.

JOHN O'DONOHUE[1]

REFERENCES

PART ONE

1. John O'Donohue, *Anam Cara: Spiritual Wisdom from the Celtic World*, Bantam, 1997, page 245.
2. From *The Works of Benjamin Franklin*, 1817.
3. Julia de Beausobre (ed.), *The Russian Letters of Spiritual Direction of Ivanov Macarios*, Moscow, 1888.
4. Sister Wendy Becket, *Meditations on Joy*, Dorling Kindersley, 1995.
5. Marie Belloc-Lowndes, *My Life and Letters*, London, 1971.
6. This section is drawn from Stephen Grabow, *Christopher Alexander – the Search for a New Paradigm in Architecture*, Oriel Press, 1983.
7. First published in 1937. Reissued in 1999 by Hodder & Stoughton.
8. From Sermon 5, a translation from the Latin. See G.S.M. Walker (ed.), *Sancti Columbani Opera*, Dublin Institute for Advanced Studies, 1970, page 84.
9. Alistair Maclean, *Hebridean Altars*, The Moray Press, 1937, page 70.
10. Words from David Adam, *The Edge of Glory*, Triangle/SPCK, 1985, page 106.
11. From *Bowthorpe News* 2000. Used by permission.
12. Sulpicius Severus, 'The Life of St Martin', in *Early Christian Lives*, Penguin Classics, 1998.
13. David Blaine's story was reported in the *Daily Mail*, 28 November 2000.
14. W.H. Lewis (ed.), *The Letters of C.S. Lewis*, London, 1966.
15. Kahlil Gibran, *The Prophet*, Heinemann, 1997, page 94.
16. The full story is told in Marie de Hennezel, *Intimate Death*, Warner, 1997, pages 179–80.

PART TWO

1. Glenn Clark is the founder of CFO (Camps Farthest Out) International, Route 1, Box 241, Walla Walla, Washington 99362, USA. This quote comes from the leaflet 'The Divine Plan'.
2. From *The Diaries of Anaïs Nin, Volume* 2.
3. Kahlil Gibran, *The Prophet*, page 61.
4. From John Bell, *The Last Journey: Reflections for the Time of Grieving*, Gia Publications USA, 1996, © Wild Goose Resources Group.
5. In *A Book of Condolences*, Azure, 1999, page 179.

6. Victor Frankl, *Man's Search for Meaning: An Introduction to Logotherapy*, Beacon Press, 1965.

PART THREE

1. *The Week*, 30 September 2000.
2. Elisabeth Kübler-Ross, *On Death and Dying*, Tavistock, 1970.
3. C.S. Lewis, *A Grief Observed*, Faber & Faber, 1966.
4. From a booklet published by Frank Rowland.
5. Information about woodland burial grounds in the UK and USA is included in N. Alberg, *The New Natural Death Handbook*, Third Revised Edition, Rider, 2000, Chapter 6.
6. This was sent to *The Friend* magazine in London and published in its 9 August 1946 edition.
7. From *Scott's Last Expedition: Captain Scott's Own Story*, London, 1923.
8. From the anthology *Dying We Live*, London, 1956.
9. Reported in the *Daily Mail Weekend Magazine*, 21 October 2000.
10. Alexander Carmichael (compiler), *Carmina Gadelica*, 1940. Scottish Academic Press, 1940, reprinted 1976.
11. Words of George Appleton, inspired by Rabindranath Tagore in *Journey for a Soul*, Collins/Fontana, 1974.

PART FOUR

1. Words from David Adam, *The Edge of Glory*, page 106.
2. John Bell, *The Last Journey: Reflections for the Time of Grieving*.
3. Alexander Carmichael (compiler), *Carmina Gadelica*, Scottish Academic Press, 1940, reprinted 1976.
4. J. Philip Newell, *Celtic Benediction*, Canterbury Press, 2000, page 80.
5. Bishop Mael, Celtic Orthodox Church, Brittany. Used with permission.
6. Scottish Academic Press Edition, 1940, reprinted 1976.
7. Used with permission of Kevin Mayhew Ltd.
8. Used with permission.
9. Anita Barrows and Joanna Macy (trans.), *Rilke's Book of Hours – Love Poems to God*, Riverhead Books, 1996.
10. Kahlil Gibran, *The Prophet*, page 94.
11. St Michael's Cottage Crafts, Bowthorpe Hall Road, Bowthorpe, Norwich NR5 9AA, UK. Telephone: 01603 746106.

PART FIVE

1. Henri Nouwen, *Our Greatest Gift – A Meditation on Dying and Caring*, HarperSanFrancisco, 1994.
2. Teilhard de Chardin, *Hymn of the Universe*, Harper & Row, 1965.
3. Michel Quoist, *Prayers of Life*, Gill and Son, 1965, page 30.
4. This is the Community of Aidan and Hilda, The Open Gate, Holy Island, Berwick-upon-Tweed TD15 2SD. Telephone: 01289 389222. E-mail: enquiries@aidan.ndo.co.uk. Website: www.aidan.org.uk
5. George McLeod, *The Whole Earth Shall Cry Glory*, Wild Goose Publications, 1985, page 60.
6. Ibid.
7. C.S. Lewis, *The Last Battle*, Bodley Head, 1956, page 183.
8. Bede, *The Ecclesiastical History of the English People, Book 5*, Oxford University Press, 1994, Chapter 12.
9. Raymond Moody, *Life after Life*, Mockingbird Books, 1975.
10. Betty Eadie, *Embraced by the Light: What Happens when You Die?*, HarperCollins, 1994.
11. From Hilary Beasley CR, *The Best Is Yet to Be*, quoted in *Hatch, Match, Despatch*, an anthology published by The Mothers' Union of Norwich Diocese in 1980, page 44.
12. This credal belief is based on the teaching of St Paul in 1 Corinthians 15:42–4.
13. Caitlin Matthews, *The Celtic Book of the Dead*, St Martin's Press, 1992.
14. Malcolm Muggeridge, *Jesus Rediscovered*, Fontana, 1969, page 57.

PART SIX

1. See *Early Christian Writings*, Penguin Classics, 1980.
2. See Adomnan of Iona, *Life of St Columba*, Penguin Classics, 1995, page 227.
3. Quoted in Ray Simpson, *Celtic Daily Light*, Hodder & Stoughton, 1999, reading for 5 November.
4. Paraphrase based on Bede's 'Life of Cuthbert' in *The Age of Bede*, Penguin Classics, 1985, page 93.
5. Paraphrase based on Bede's *The Ecclesiastical History of the English People*, page 214.
6. Recorded by a monk in Bede's monastery named Cuthbert, as *Cuthbert's Letter on the Death of Bede*.
7. The story is told in Marie de Hennezel, *Intimate Death: How the Dying Teach Us to Live*.
8. Text used by permission of Stainer and Bell.

9. Nigel spent his last weeks in my home, and I believe he wanted the discovery of his 'heavenly career' to be widely shared. His story is told under the pseudonym 'Bruce' in Sally Simpson, *Bruce: Patience Please, I Think I'm Melting*, New Millennium, 1997, available from The Hobby Horse, Saint Michael's Cottage Crafts, Bowthorpe, Norwich NR5 9AA, UK. Telephone: 01603 746106.

SOME HELPFUL BOOKS

N. Alberg, *The New Natural Death Handbook*, Rider, 2000

John Bell, *The Last Journey: Reflections for the Time of Grieving*, Gia Publications, USA, 1996, cassette and/or book

Maggie Callanan and Patricia Kelley, *Final Gifts: Understanding and Helping the Dying*, Hodder & Stoughton, 1992

Common Worship: Pastoral Services, Church House Press, 2000

Michael Dunn, *The Good Death Guide*, Pathways, 2000

Betty J. Eadie, *Embraced by the Light: What Happens When You Die?*, HarperCollins, 1994

Rachel Harding and Mary Dyson (eds), *A Book of Condolences: Classic Letters of Bereavement*, Azure, 1999

Ted Harrison, *Beyond Dying: The Mystery of Eternity*, Lion, 2000

Marie de Hennezel, *Intimate Death: How the Dying Teach Us to Live*, Warner Books, 1998

Elisabeth Kübler-Ross, *On Death and Dying*, Tavistock, 1970

Carol Neiman and Emily Goldman, *Afterlife: The Complete Guide to Life after Death*, Boxtree, 1994

S.B. Nuland, *How we Die*, Vintage, 1997

John O'Donohue, *Anam Cara: Spiritual Wisdom from the Celtic World*, Bantam, 1997

K.D. Singh, *The Grace in Dying*, Newleaf, 1998

Dr Tony Walter, *Funerals and How to Improve Them*, Hodder & Stoughton, 1990

OTHER BOOKS BY RAY SIMPSON

Published by St Aidan Press: *Give Yourself a Retreat on Holy Island*

Published by Hodder & Stoughton: *Celtic Blessings for Everyday* (this includes prayers for funerals, loss and bereavement)

Celtic Daily Light (this includes readings on death and the afterlife)

Exploring Celtic Spirituality: Historic Roots for our Future (this includes a chapter on triumphant dying)

Soulfriendship: Celtic Insights into Spiritual Mentoring (this includes a chapter on soul friends at death)

Celtic Worship through the Year (this includes liturgies celebrating the anniversaries of saints' deaths)

PULL-OUT FORMS

These forms are for you to complete and keep in a safe place.
Make photocopies, or buy extra copies of this book to give to
those who will need this information.

FORM I
ON MY DEATHBED

Instructions to my nearest relative
(delete or leave blank as necessary).

I would like a visit from a minister: Yes/No

Name of minister:
Address and telephone number:

Please also contact:

Telephone number:

I would like to receive the following ministries
(tick or circle as appropriate):
Prayer/ Holy Communion/Anointing/Confession
Other (please state):

I would also like the following:

[a] Favourite Bible passages read:

[b] Hymns/songs sung:

[c] Prayers/poems read:

[d] Music played:

FORM 2
TO FIND WHEN I DIE

(Fill in or leave blank as appropriate.)

My name:

My address:

The following documents are kept in:
(add names, addresses and account details of banks, building societies, etc.)

Insurance policies (add name and address of broker):

Investment details (add name and address of company):

Details of where any documents can be found in my house or on my computer:

House/mortgage papers:

Pension/benefit details/certificates:

Birth/marriage certificates:

Credit/hire purchase commitments:

Credit/debit card details:

Annual registrations (TV, MOT, car tax, etc.):

House (valuation):

Money/cash:

Contents of house valuation:

Jewellery details and valuation:

Anything else of value:

My solicitor is:
(add name, address, telephone number)

My will is stored at:

For financial affairs contact:

In order to save yourself the distress of dealing with unwanted commercial mail, e-mail and phone calls to me after my death, write to The Bereavement Register, 50 London Road, Sevenoaks, Kent TN3 1AS, or telephone The Bereavement Register Helpline on 01732 46000. Give them my full names, address and date of death and ask them to remove my details from all marketing databases.

Other instructions:

FORM 3
MY WILL

The checklist for points to include in your will should cover the following:

House (plus valuation)
Money/cash
Contents of house
Bank/building society accounts
Investments
Insurance policies
Pensions
Death benefits (jewellery or other valuable objects)
Anything else of value

MY FUNERAL ARRANGEMENTS

Instructions to my closest relative or executor.

My full names:

My address:

Date of birth:

Name, address and telephone number of my doctor:

Please contact the minister of my church before making other arrangements. Name and address of the minister:

I wish my funeral to take place at the following church/chapel/crematorium:

I wish my body to be taken into church a day/half-day before the funeral, so that it may rest there and others may be near it.
(Please tick if desired.)

I wish my body to be buried/cremated at:

I wish my ashes to be buried/scattered at:

I wish the following funeral directors to be contacted:

My choice of hymns is:

My choice of music is:

My choice of readings/poems is:

I would like the following person/people to speak or take part:

I would prefer donations to flowers/I would like any flowers to go with my body to the cemetery/remain in the church/be given to the following people (delete and add details as necessary):

Please tell the following of the funeral beforehand (add names, addresses and telephone numbers):

Other notes: